Copyright © by EdgeSavvy LLC

All rights reserved. This book or parts thereof may not be reproduced in any form, stored in any retrieval system, or transmitted in any form by any means—electronic, mechanical, photocopy, recording, or otherwise—without prior written permission of the publisher, except as provided by United States of America copyright law and fair use. For permission requests, write to the publisher at info@edgesavvy.com

ISBN 979-8486138744

Images used under license of Canva.com

Disclaimer: The contents of this book are for informational purposes only and are not a substitute for professional medical advice, diagnosis, or treatment. Always consult with a qualified medical professional for diagnosis and treatment of health or mental concerns. Any decisions you make, and the consequences thereof are your own. Under no circumstances can you hold EdgeSavvy, author or publisher liable for any actions that you take.

Our books may be purchased in bulk for promotional, educational or business use. Please contact the publisher with inquiries.

MY FUTURE
DEPENDS ON
WHAT I DO AND
FOCUS ON NEXT

Claim **BADASS YOU**

A Journal - Workbook For Women To Get To Know Yourself, Unleash The Power Within, Release Self-Doubt & Become A Conscious Creator Of Your Life

50 Positive Affirmations & 200 Unique Self-Exploration Prompts

Welcome to discovering and claiming the NEW TRUE YOU! Congratulations on being brave and willing to find you - the real you and start releasing the stories and blocks that you've been holding onto for years. Let them go and reclaim your power.

This is NOT your regular journal where you just journal your thoughts. This journal offers a deeper dive into the Self.

In this journal you'll find **50 powerful affirmations and 200 unique self-exploration prompts** that will help you explore who you are, your shadows, appreciate what you have, *enable* you to look deeper into yourself, and focus on the good and the things that you want to create and see in your life.

Additionally, you'll have an extra page for your thoughts, reflections, gratitude or to record your manifestations.

Why Affirmations?
Why Journaling Prompts?

Affirmations and prompts serve as guides on your journey of self-exploration and personal growth. Affirmations are positive statements that you repeat to yourself, helping you to shift your beliefs, perceptions and boost your confidence and motivation. Prompts or questions, on the other hand, encourage deep reflection. They make you think about your thoughts, feelings, and experiences, helping you to identify patterns and discover hidden aspects of yourself. When used together and in a certain way, these tools can be like a flashlight in a dark room, illuminating the path to a better understanding of who you are and the potential for positive change in your life.

We find ourselves through explorations. Sometimes we're not able to ask ourselves the right questions or guide ourselves in the right direction because we stand too close to our circumstances, thoughts, emotions, belief system, etc.

Prompts and ***Affirmations*** will help you to explore what IS, step into higher vibration, move towards and focus on your desires, and reinforce your intentions and efforts.

Every affirmation and prompt is different and unique.

Some sample prompts:

- A place that makes me feel most peaceful is...
- I can change my sadness to...
- Today I'll express my appreciation to...
- My imperfection that I want to embrace is...

HOW TO USE THIS JOURNAL

The intention of this journal is to hold space for self-exploration so you start understanding yourself, what you truly want, and even start taking inspired actions to get 'there' - to manifest what you truly desire.

You are what you think and believe in. If you think of yourself in a positive way, you will create a positive thought, which will in turn transform into a positive feeling, action, and eventually, a result. If you don't like the results - what you see in your life at this moment, this is your opportunity to explore why this happens and start shifting things.

Journaling and affirmations can help you purify your thoughts and restructure the dynamics of your brain so you can expand, grow and believe in your own power.

You'll find each affirmation on a beautiful, earthy, and calming picture, followed by four prompts and a free-flow journaling page, just like the one on the next page.

Each day read an affirmation starting with page 1 or randomly pick a page you'd like to focus on.

Now let's explore what needs to be present for affirmations to work so you see the results you desire.

Date ______________________

Today is an amazing day because ______________________

Some of the positive ways I've changed are ______________________

Someone who always makes me smile is ______________________

Today I focus on feeling ______________________

There are 3 components necessary for affirmations to work and become your new beliefs and truths:

Repetition. Repetition of affirmations helps create new memories that will later serve as a reference point for the subconscious mind when breaking negative thinking and emotional patterns. However, if you just read or say an affirmation once and do nothing else, it's not likely that it will make much difference or become your new truth. Therefore, it's necessary that you combine repetition with the next components.

A visual. Every time you say an affirmation, imagine something that would represent that affirmation - what and how you'd feel, where you'd be if the statement were true. It can be a video or a picture in your mind.

If you say "I love myself unconditionally," what would that look like, what would you do? Maybe you take a break and go for a walk, so you'd simply imagine yourself walking in a park and observing the surroundings.

An emotion. The subconscious mind doesn't quite understand and register words, but it definitely understands emotions and feelings. Therefore, you may want to create as many good emotions and feelings as possible along with the visual you're creating.

So every time you say an affirmation, not only have a visual, but also allow yourself to feel and experience things (as if you already had it).

What would it feel like to go for a walk? What would it feel like to have a breeze on your skin? How would your body feel when you take a walk on a beautiful sunny day?

Prompts are designed to help you delve deeper into your exploration journey, guiding you to focus on the positive aspects of your life, and learn more about yourself each day while inspiring action.

It will take you only a couple of minutes a day to respond to four prompts, and spending those couple minutes can kick-start your journey towards achieving your desired results. Focus on what you want to create, what you want to see in your life, who you want to be or become, and start letting go of what no longer serves you.

Because you chose to get this journal and do the work, I want to gift you "**Miracle Activator mini**" e-book absolutely FREE. You deserve this. This training will help you take things to the next level and start removing internal blocks and get closer to your desired life.

Get it here
bit.ly/MAMebook

Now... Are you ready to get to know yourself and step into your power?
Let's dive in!

I LOVE AND APPRECIATE MY BODY. MY BODY IS BEAUTIFUL AND IT ALLOWS ME TO EXPERIENCE THIS BEAUTIFUL LIFE.

Date

My intention for today is

A person that I'll always be grateful for is

One of my best qualities is

One positive habit I would like to create is

I Want to Manifest in My Life

(Describe in detail with visuals and senses)

Thoughts - Reflections - Manifestations

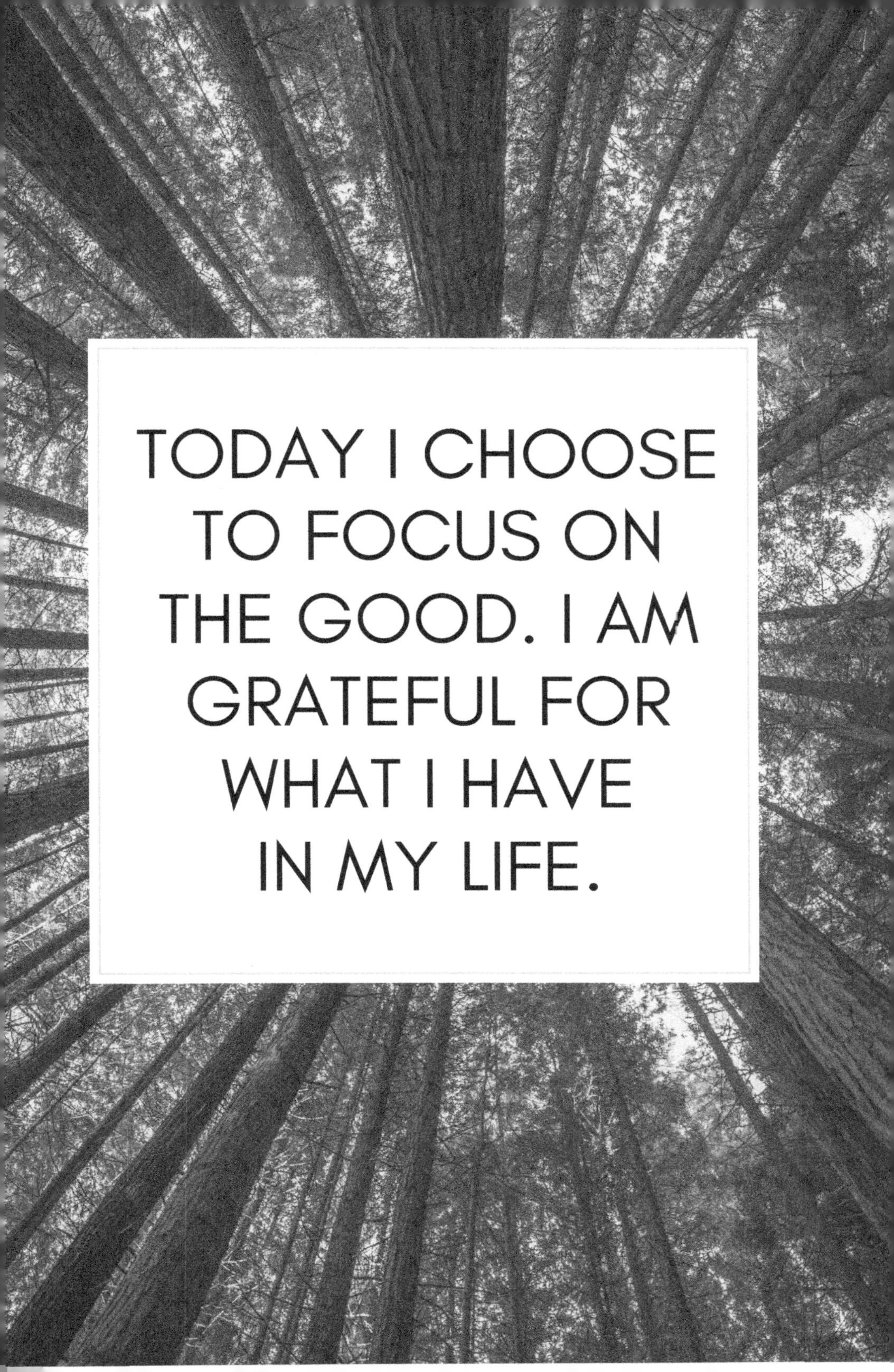
TODAY I CHOOSE
TO FOCUS ON
THE GOOD. I AM
GRATEFUL FOR
WHAT I HAVE
IN MY LIFE.

Date

Today is an amazing day because

Some of the positive ways I've changed are

Someone who always makes me smile is

Today I focus on feeling

I Want to Manifest in My Life

(Describe in detail with visuals and senses)

Thoughts - Reflections - Manifestations

I ACCEPT AND
GENUINELY
APPRECIATE EVERY
COMPLIMENT.
I AM OPEN TO
RECEIVING MY
BLESSINGS.

Date

Today the way I can fill my cup before giving myself to others is

The most beautiful quality in a person is

I deserve love because

A place where I feel happy is

I Want to Manifest in My Life

(Describe in detail with visuals and senses)

Thoughts - Reflections - Manifestations

I AM PERFECT
JUST THE WAY
I AM, AND
I CHOOSE TO
LOVE AND
APPRECIATE
MYSELF.

Date ____________________

One relationship I'd like to improve is ____________________

My best friend would describe me to a stranger as ____________________

A compliment I'd love to receive is ____________________

What I appreciate about this moment is ____________________

I Want to Manifest in My Life

(Describe in detail with visuals and senses)

Thoughts - Reflections - Manifestations

I HAVE THE ABILITY TO OVERCOME ANY CHALLENGES IN MY LIFE. THEY ARE THE STEPPING STONES TOWARDS BETTER THINGS.

Date ______________________

I love myself most because ______________________

A friend I'd like to catch up with is ______________________

Today I celebrate ______________________

One thing I can do today to take care of my body is ______________________

I Want to Manifest in My Life

(Describe in detail with visuals and senses)

Thoughts ~ Reflections ~ Manifestations

I CHOOSE TO SEE THE POSITIVE EVEN IN TOUGH TIMES. THERE IS A LESSON IN EVERYTHING AND THAT THOSE LESSONS HELP ME GROW.

Date

I feel happiest when

Something I'd love to do more of every day is

An affirmation that will help me today is

My top three priorities are

I Want to Manifest in My Life

(Describe in detail with visuals and senses)

Thoughts - Reflections - Manifestations

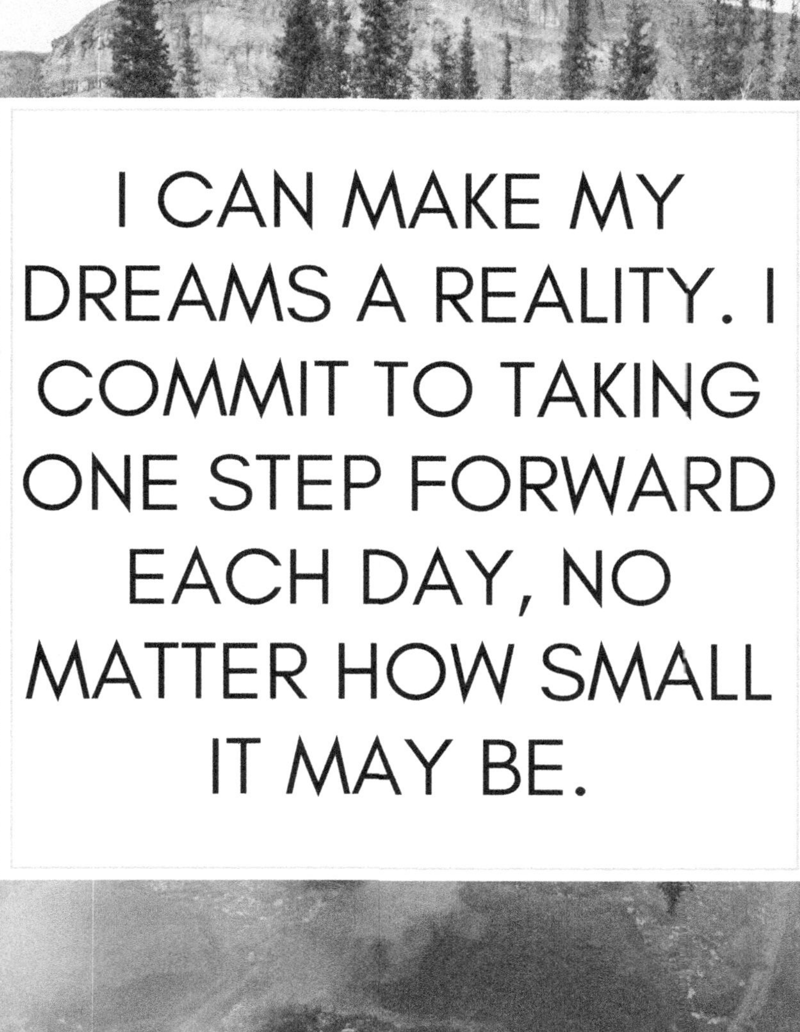
I CAN MAKE MY DREAMS A REALITY. I COMMIT TO TAKING ONE STEP FORWARD EACH DAY, NO MATTER HOW SMALL IT MAY BE.

Date

What I need the most today is

One thing I will do today to feel more joy is

Something that makes me feel safe is

My biggest dream is

I Want to Manifest in My Life

(Describe in detail with visuals and senses)

Thoughts - Reflections - Manifestations

I ALWAYS FOLLOW
MY HEART, AND IT
LEADS ME TO
BEAUTIFUL
EXPERIENCES.

Date

Music that lifts me up & makes me feel happy is

One thing I can do today to love myself more is

My ideal day is

When I go to bed I want to feel

I Want to Manifest in My Life

(Describe in detail with visuals and senses)

Thoughts ~ Reflections ~ Manifestations

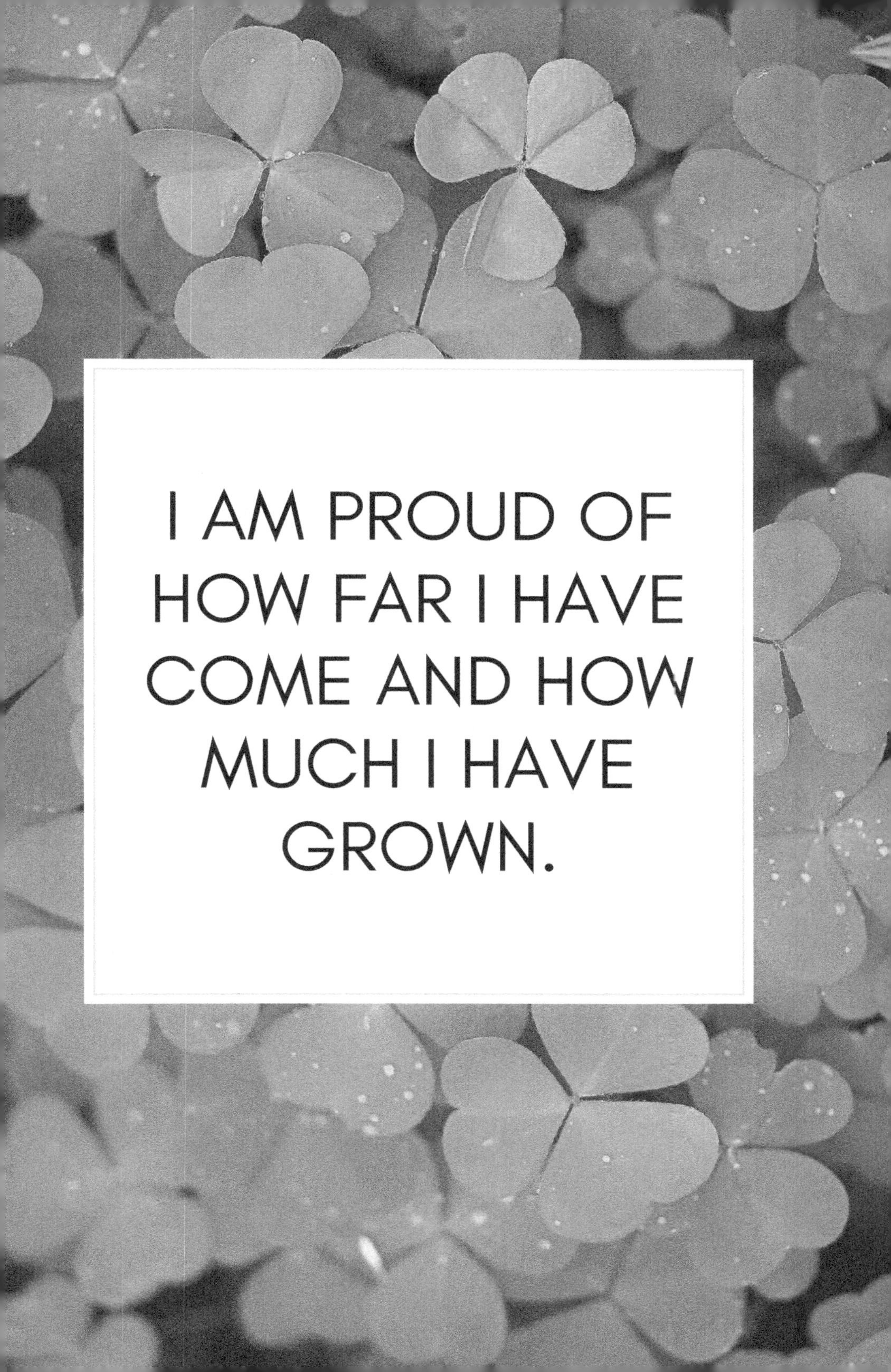
I AM PROUD OF
HOW FAR I HAVE
COME AND HOW
MUCH I HAVE
GROWN.

Date

The word of the day is

The last time I truly felt at peace

Today I am excited about

My favorite way of self-care is

I Want to Manifest in My Life

(Describe in detail with visuals and senses)

Thoughts - Reflections - Manifestations

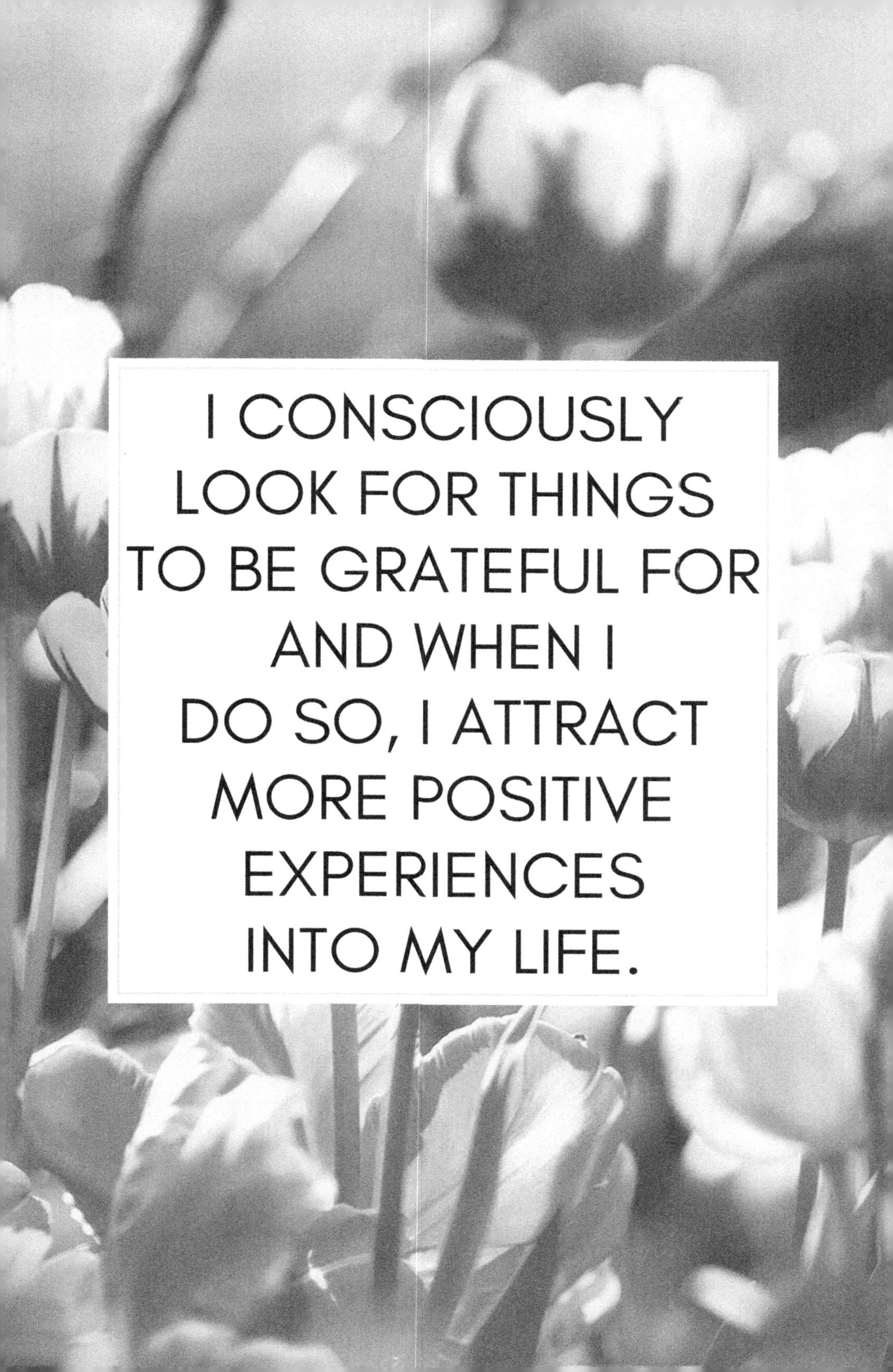
I CONSCIOUSLY
LOOK FOR THINGS
TO BE GRATEFUL FOR
AND WHEN I
DO SO, I ATTRACT
MORE POSITIVE
EXPERIENCES
INTO MY LIFE.

Date ______________________

Something that makes me feel good no matter what is

A person that I'm grateful to have in my life is

Three words that describe my style are

A tradition I love and look forward every year is

I Want to Manifest in My Life

(Describe in detail with visuals and senses)

Thoughts - Reflections - Manifestations

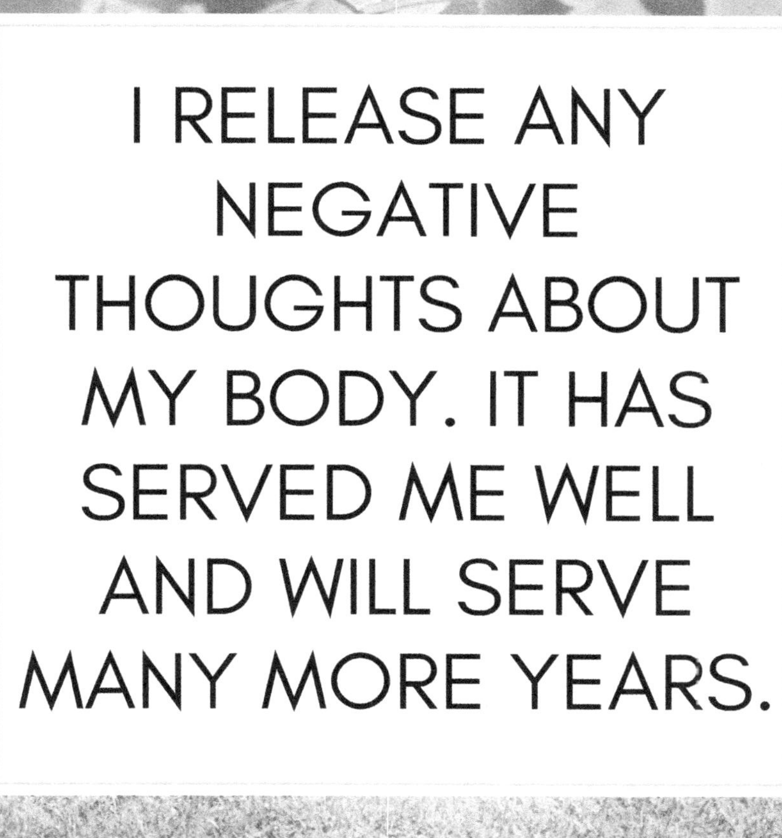
I RELEASE ANY NEGATIVE THOUGHTS ABOUT MY BODY. IT HAS SERVED ME WELL AND WILL SERVE MANY MORE YEARS.

Date

One positive thing my past taught me is

I feel loved when

My favorite smell is

One thing I will do today to appreciate people in my life is

I Want to Manifest in My Life

(Describe in detail with visuals and senses)

Thoughts - Reflections - Manifestations

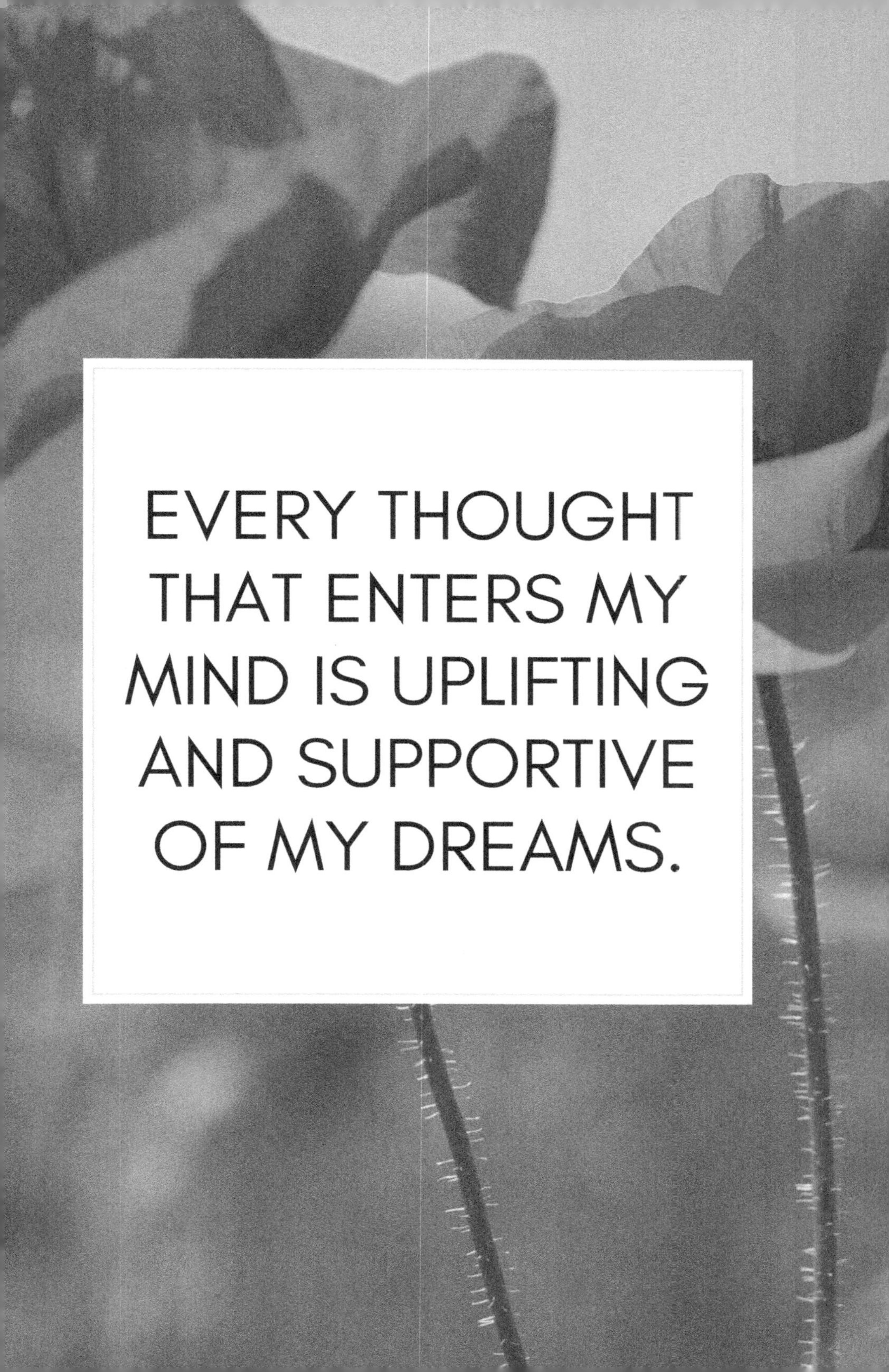
EVERY THOUGHT
THAT ENTERS MY
MIND IS UPLIFTING
AND SUPPORTIVE
OF MY DREAMS.

Date

My greatest strength is

Things I love about my family are

A time I don't want to forget is

I am cultivating more joy in my life by

I Want to Manifest in My Life

(Describe in detail with visuals and senses)

Thoughts - Reflections - Manifestations

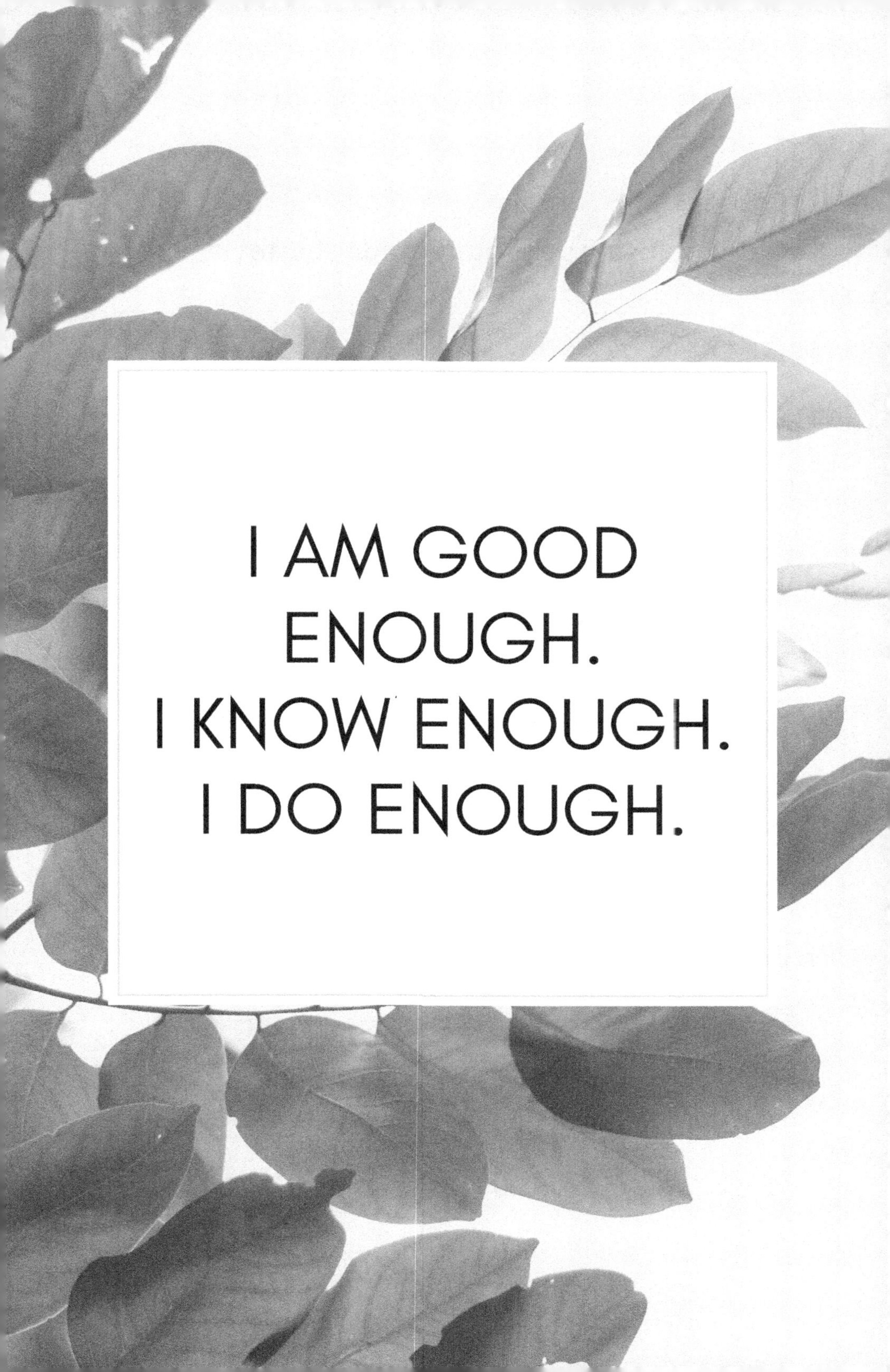
I AM GOOD
ENOUGH.
I KNOW ENOUGH.
I DO ENOUGH.

Date

Something I could do to start my day better is

I can be kinder to myself by

Something beautiful outside my window is

A project that I look forward to finishing this month is

I Want to Manifest in My Life

(Describe in detail with visuals and senses)

Thoughts - Reflections - Manifestations

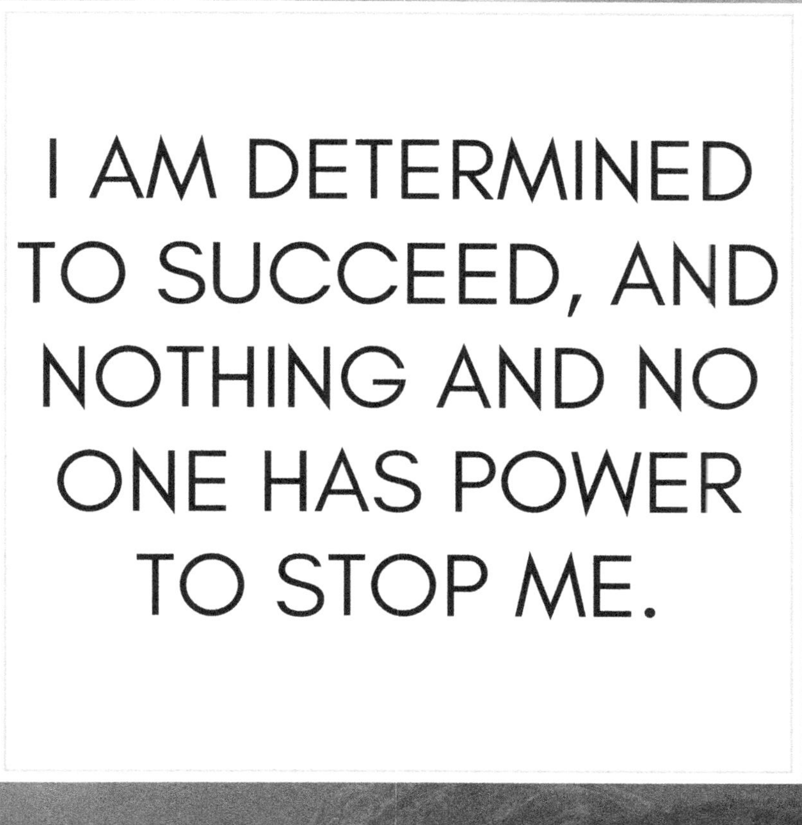

I AM DETERMINED TO SUCCEED, AND NOTHING AND NO ONE HAS POWER TO STOP ME.

Date

Something (or someone) I am very proud of is

When I wake in the morning I want to feel

Something that I look forward to this week

A quote that inspires me

I Want to Manifest in My Life

(Describe in detail with visuals and senses)

Thoughts - Reflections - Manifestations

I LOVE MYSELF UNCONDITIONALLY, WITH ALL IMPERFECTIONS AND FLAWS. I AM IMPERFECTLY PERFECT.

Date ______________________

My favorite experience in the past year was ______________________

Something I can do today to get closer to my goals is ______________________

Someone who is always kind to me is ______________________

Today three things I am most grateful for are ______________________

I Want to Manifest in My Life

(Describe in detail with visuals and senses)

Thoughts - Reflections - Manifestations

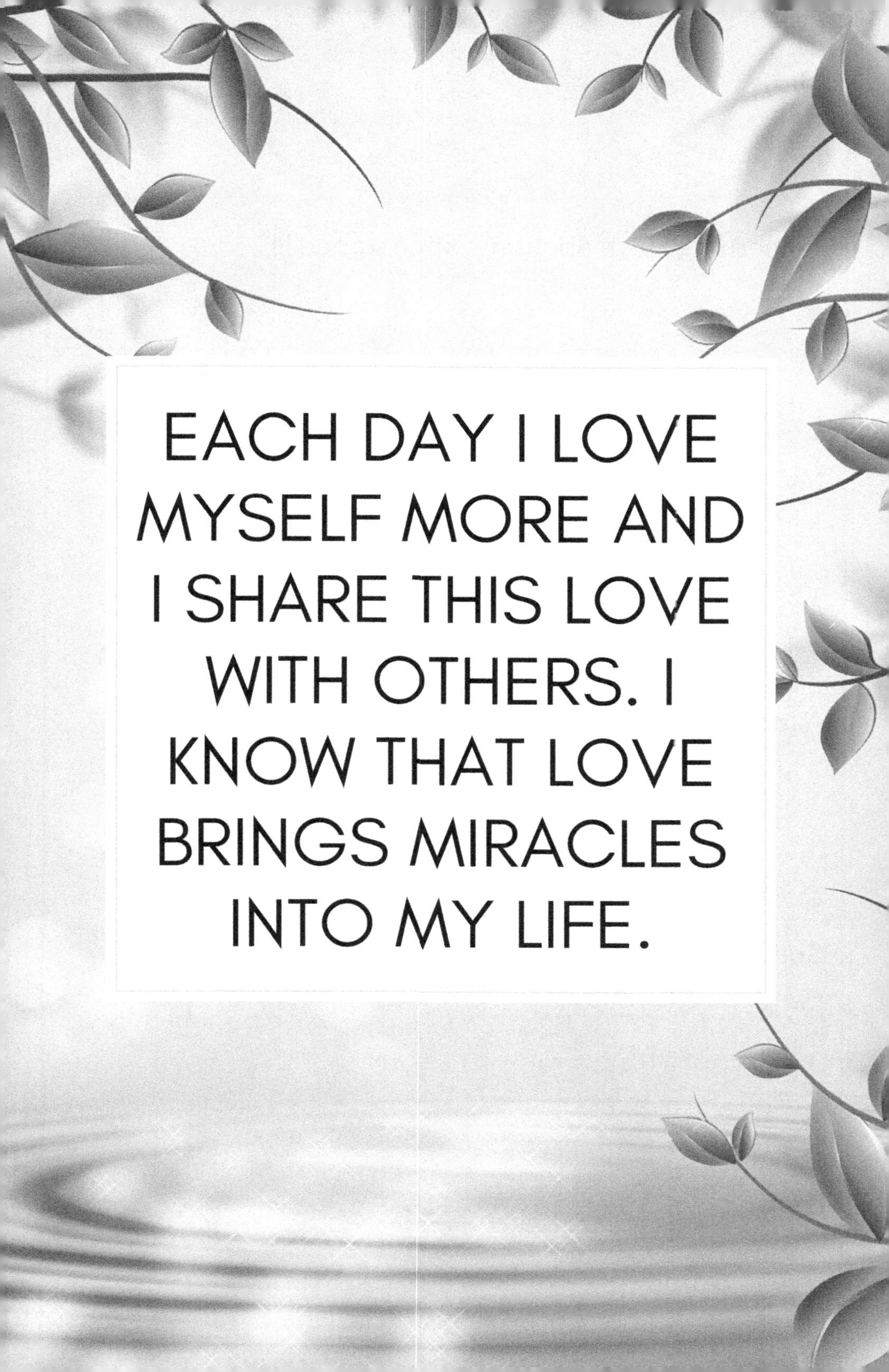
EACH DAY I LOVE
MYSELF MORE AND
I SHARE THIS LOVE
WITH OTHERS. I
KNOW THAT LOVE
BRINGS MIRACLES
INTO MY LIFE.

Date

Something I love about my appearance is

My main goal today is

A mistake that helped me grow is

Something that makes me feel confident is

I Want to Manifest in My Life

(Describe in detail with visuals and senses)

Thoughts - Reflections - Manifestations

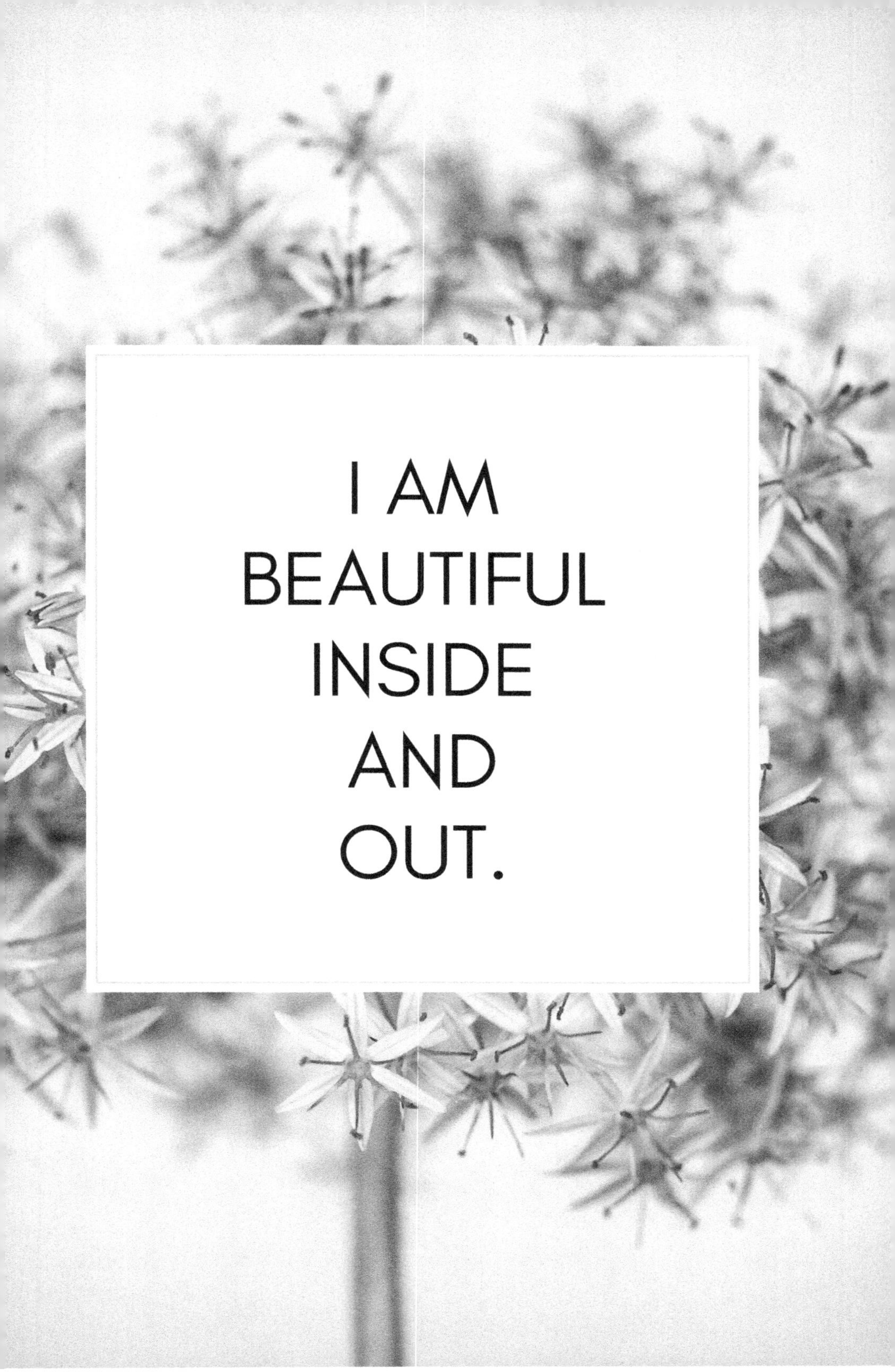
I AM
BEAUTIFUL
INSIDE
AND
OUT.

Date

Something that makes me smile is

I am willing to let go of

Things I'll do today to improve myself are

Three things I'll do today to get closer to my desires are

I Want to Manifest in My Life

(Describe in detail with visuals and senses)

Thoughts ~ Reflections ~ Manifestations

I AM LOVED AND
ACCEPTED BY
OTHERS AND
BY MYSEL.

Date ______________________

I would like to make more time for ______________________

Right this moment I feel ______________________

My best quality is ______________________

Something that is very important to me ______________________

I Want to Manifest in My Life

(Describe in detail with visuals and senses)

Thoughts - Reflections - Manifestations

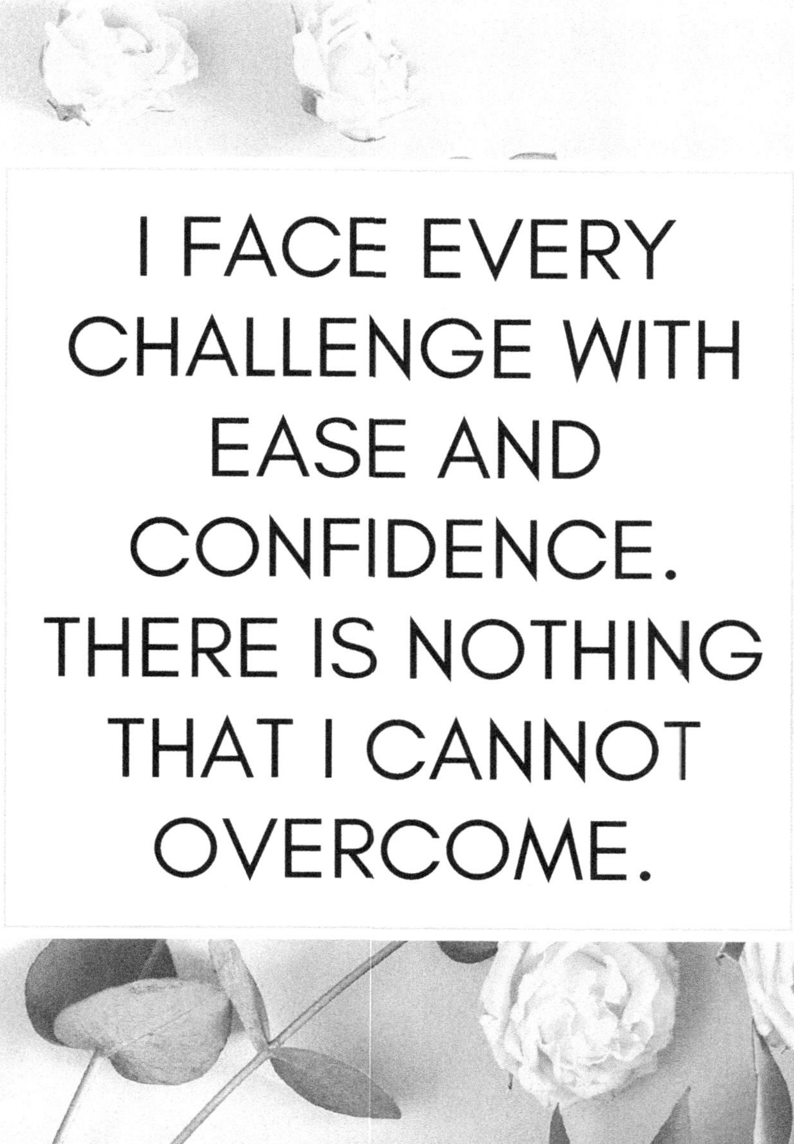

I FACE EVERY CHALLENGE WITH EASE AND CONFIDENCE. THERE IS NOTHING THAT I CANNOT OVERCOME.

Date

I am a good person because

The last compliment I received was

One of the ways I can appreciate my mistakes is

Something that would help me have a better night sleep is

I Want to Manifest in My Life

(Describe in detail with visuals and senses)

Thoughts - Reflections - Manifestations

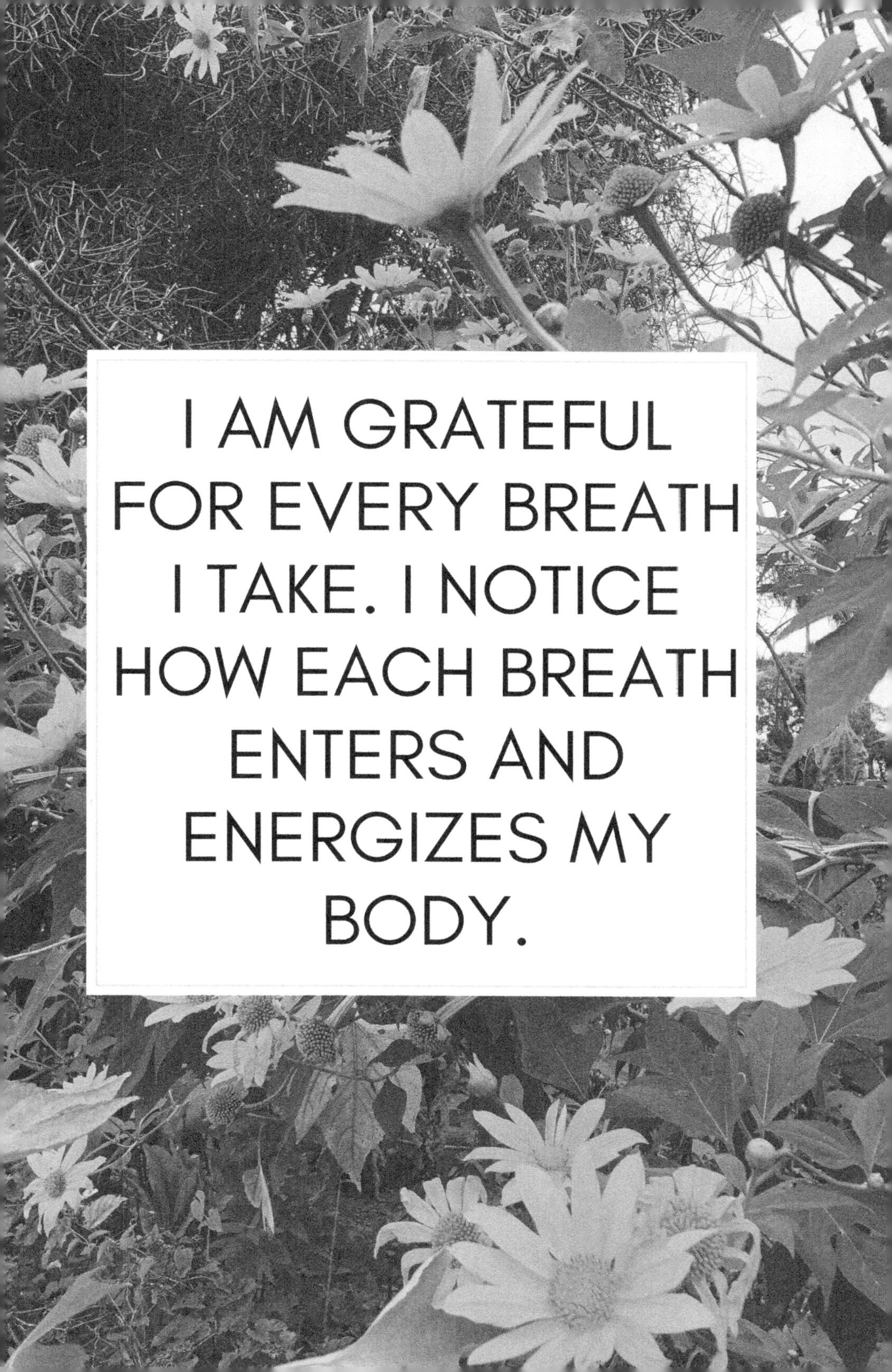
I AM GRATEFUL
FOR EVERY BREATH
I TAKE. I NOTICE
HOW EACH BREATH
ENTERS AND
ENERGIZES MY
BODY.

Date ______________________

This week the biggest thing I accomplished is ______________________

I would describe myself to someone as ______________________

I love life because ______________________

One way I can improve my relationship with my family is

I Want to Manifest in My Life

(Describe in detail with visuals and senses)

Thoughts - Reflections - Manifestations

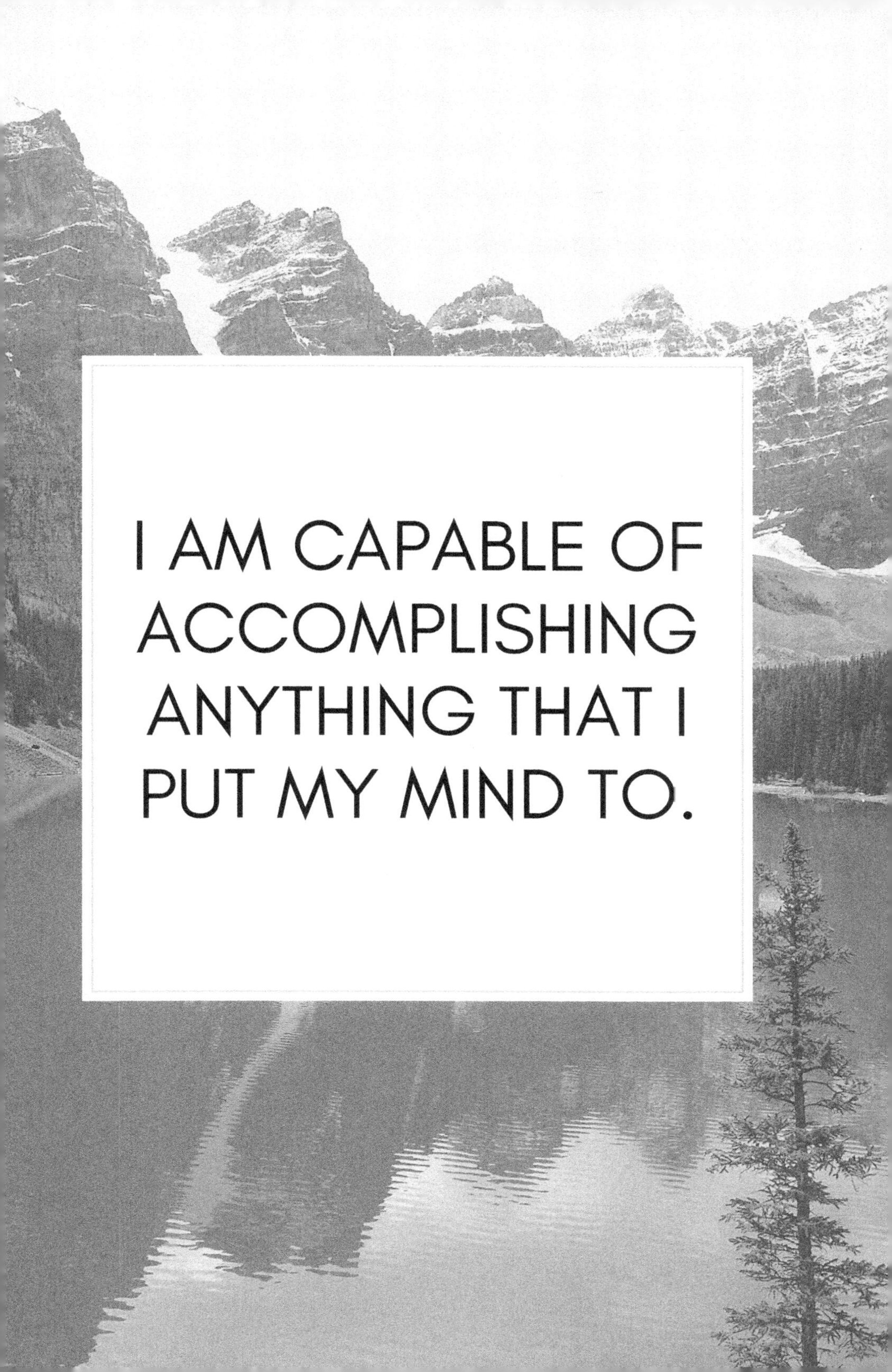
I AM CAPABLE OF ACCOMPLISHING ANYTHING THAT I PUT MY MIND TO.

Date ______________________

I enjoy spending time with ______________________

I can improve my health by ______________________

Something I am really good at is ______________________

A challenge I would like to tackle is ______________________

I Want to Manifest in My Life

(Describe in detail with visuals and senses)

Thoughts - Reflections - Manifestations

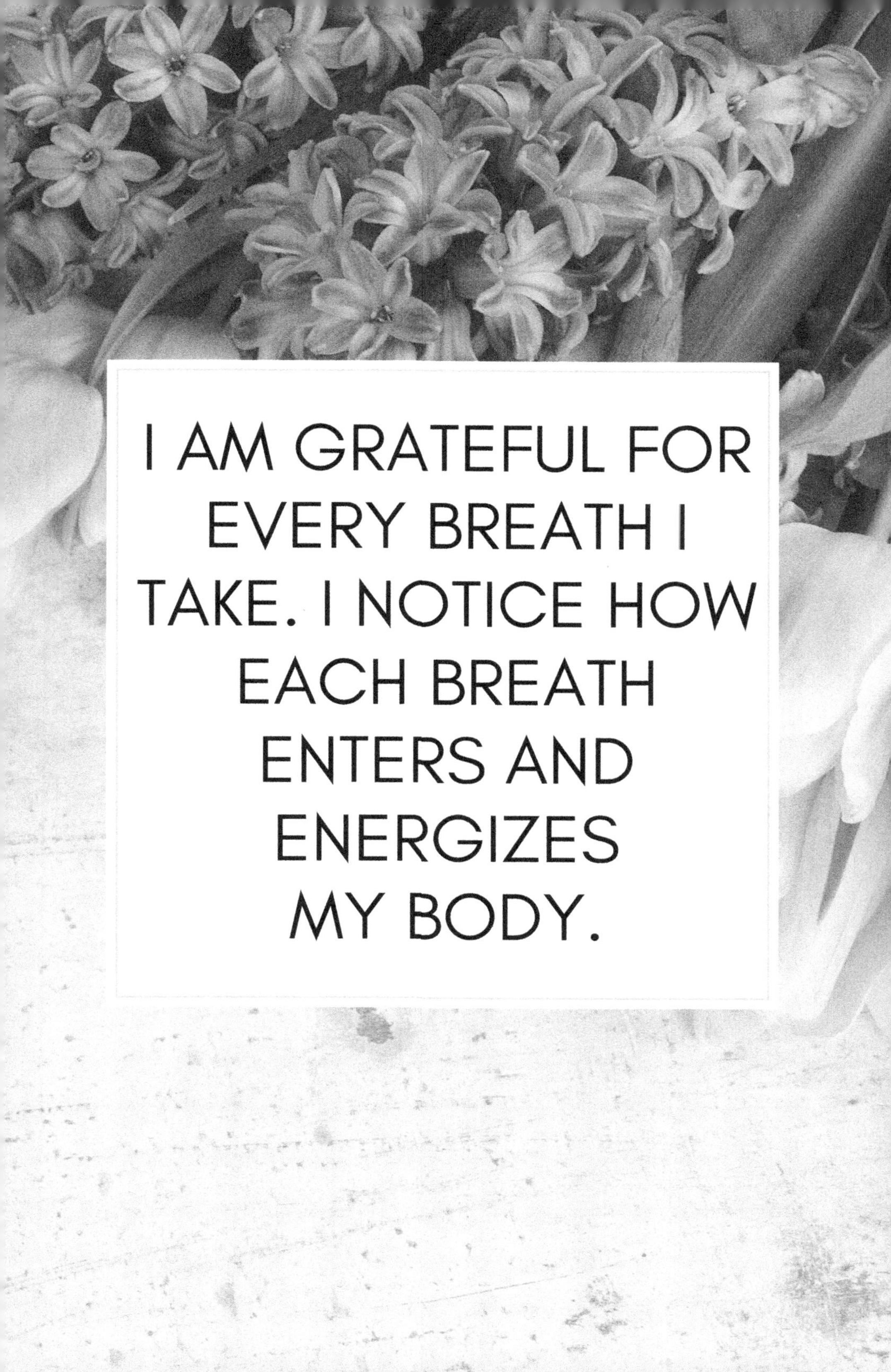
I AM GRATEFUL FOR
EVERY BREATH I
TAKE. I NOTICE HOW
EACH BREATH
ENTERS AND
ENERGIZES
MY BODY.

Date

I am most confident when

Five favorite things about myself are

I am lovable because

Something I want people to say about me when I'm not around is

I Want to Manifest in My Life

(Describe in detail with visuals and senses)

Thoughts - Reflections - Manifestations

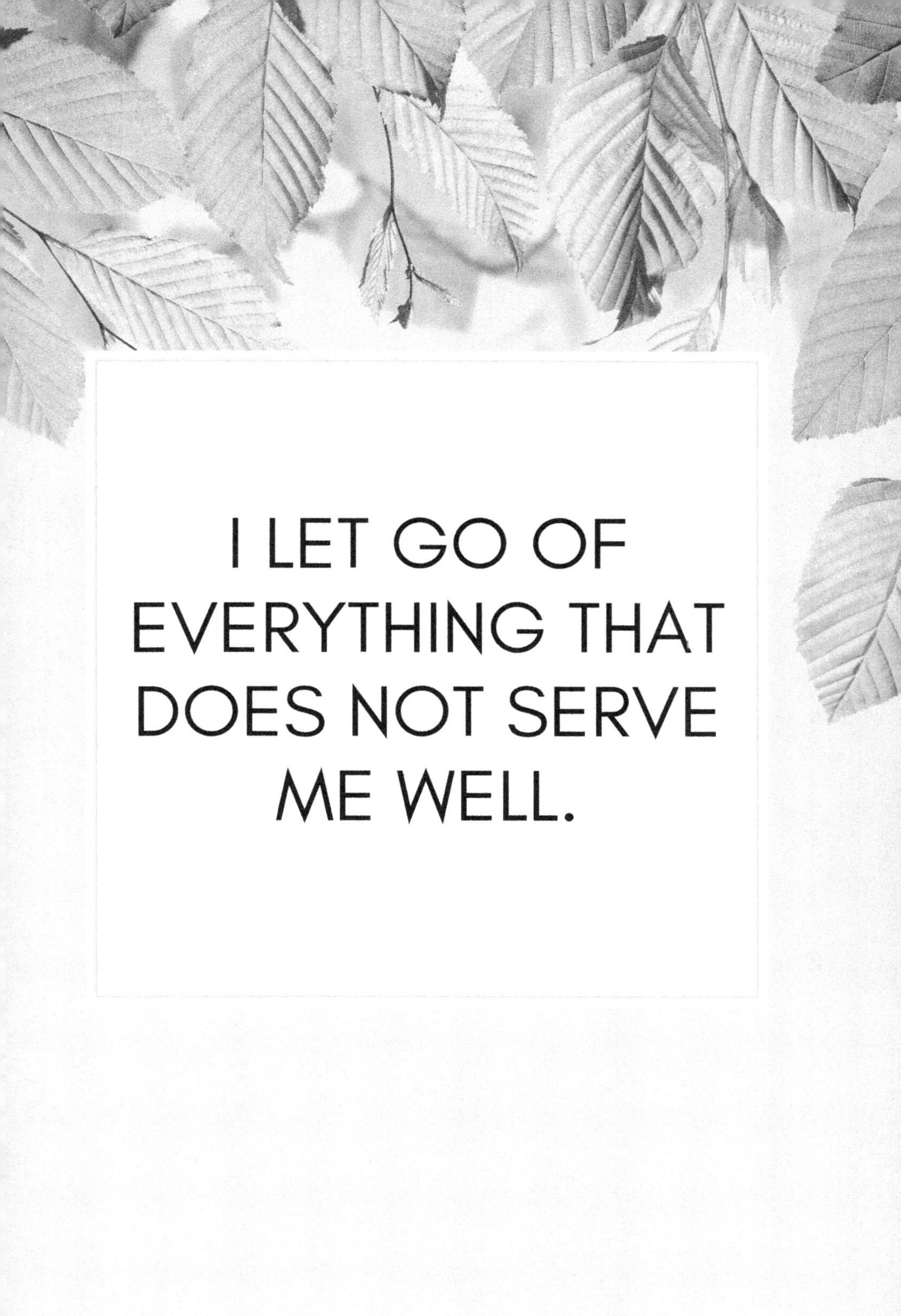

I LET GO OF EVERYTHING THAT DOES NOT SERVE ME WELL.

Date ______________________

I always have fun when ______________________

I can change my negative self-talk by ______________________

Something new I would like to try is ______________________

One thing I can do today to feel more peaceful is ______________________

I Want to Manifest in My Life

(Describe in detail with visuals and senses)

Thoughts ~ Reflections ~ Manifestations

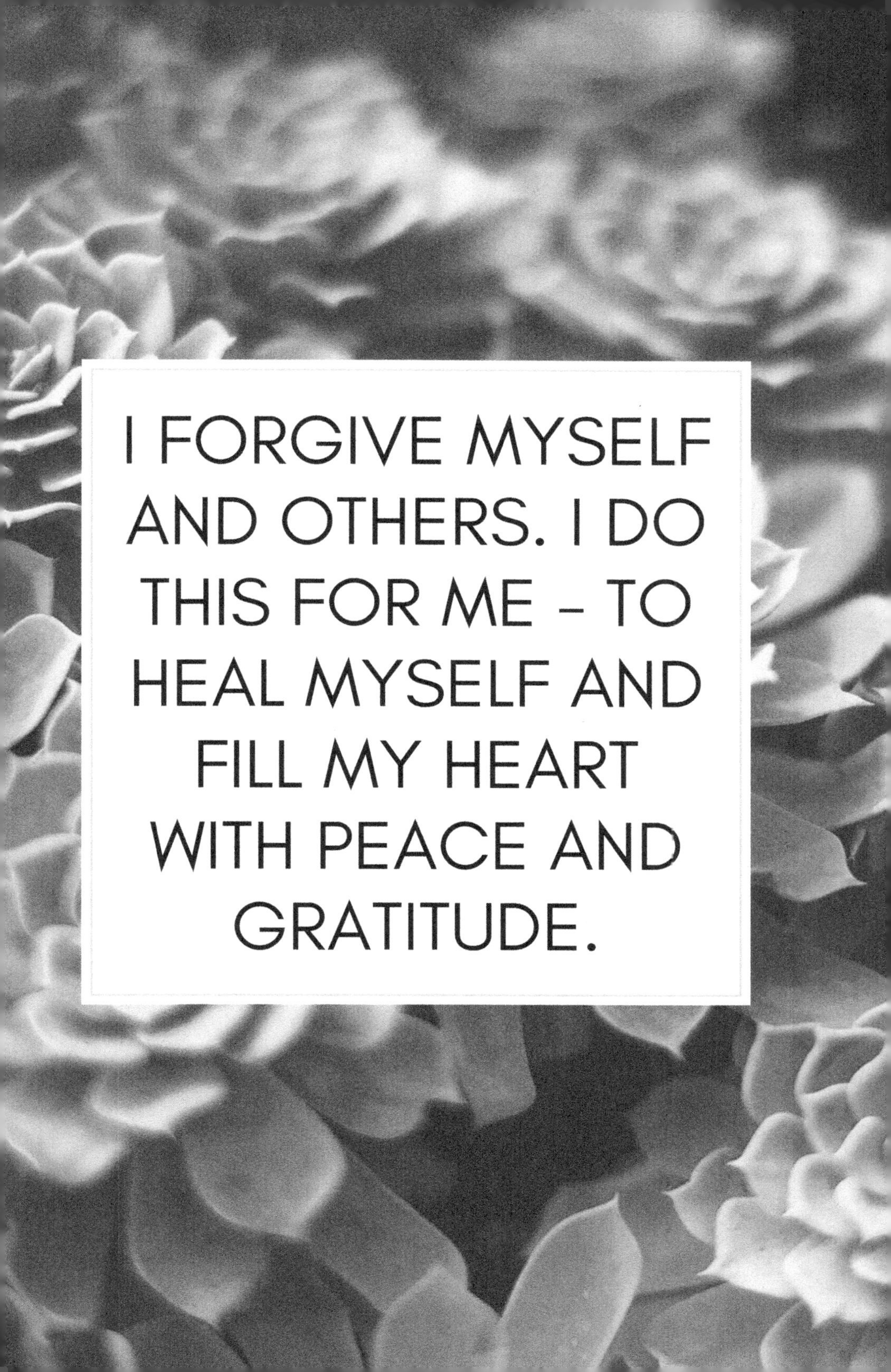
I FORGIVE MYSELF AND OTHERS. I DO THIS FOR ME – TO HEAL MYSELF AND FILL MY HEART WITH PEACE AND GRATITUDE.

Date

If money wasn't an issue, I would

Something that makes me feel fulfilled and satisfied is

If I were to write a love note to myself, it would say

I feel abundant when

I Want to Manifest in My Life

(Describe in detail with visuals and senses)

Thoughts - Reflections - Manifestations

I TRUST MYSELF
AND MY ABILITY
TO MAKE GREAT
DECISIONS.

Date

The greatest gift in my life is

The accomplishment that I am most proud of is

Today I let go of

I choose peace and happiness, even if

I Want to Manifest in My Life

(Describe in detail with visuals and senses)

Thoughts ~ Reflections ~ Manifestations

I ATTRACT LOVING
AND UPLIFTING
PEOPLE INTO MY
LIFE, AND I'M
GRATEFUL FOR
THAT.

Date

My best quality is

My biggest dream is

One thing I will show love for myself was

Today I choose to focus on

I Want to Manifest in My Life

(Describe in detail with visuals and senses)

Thoughts ~ Reflections ~ Manifestations

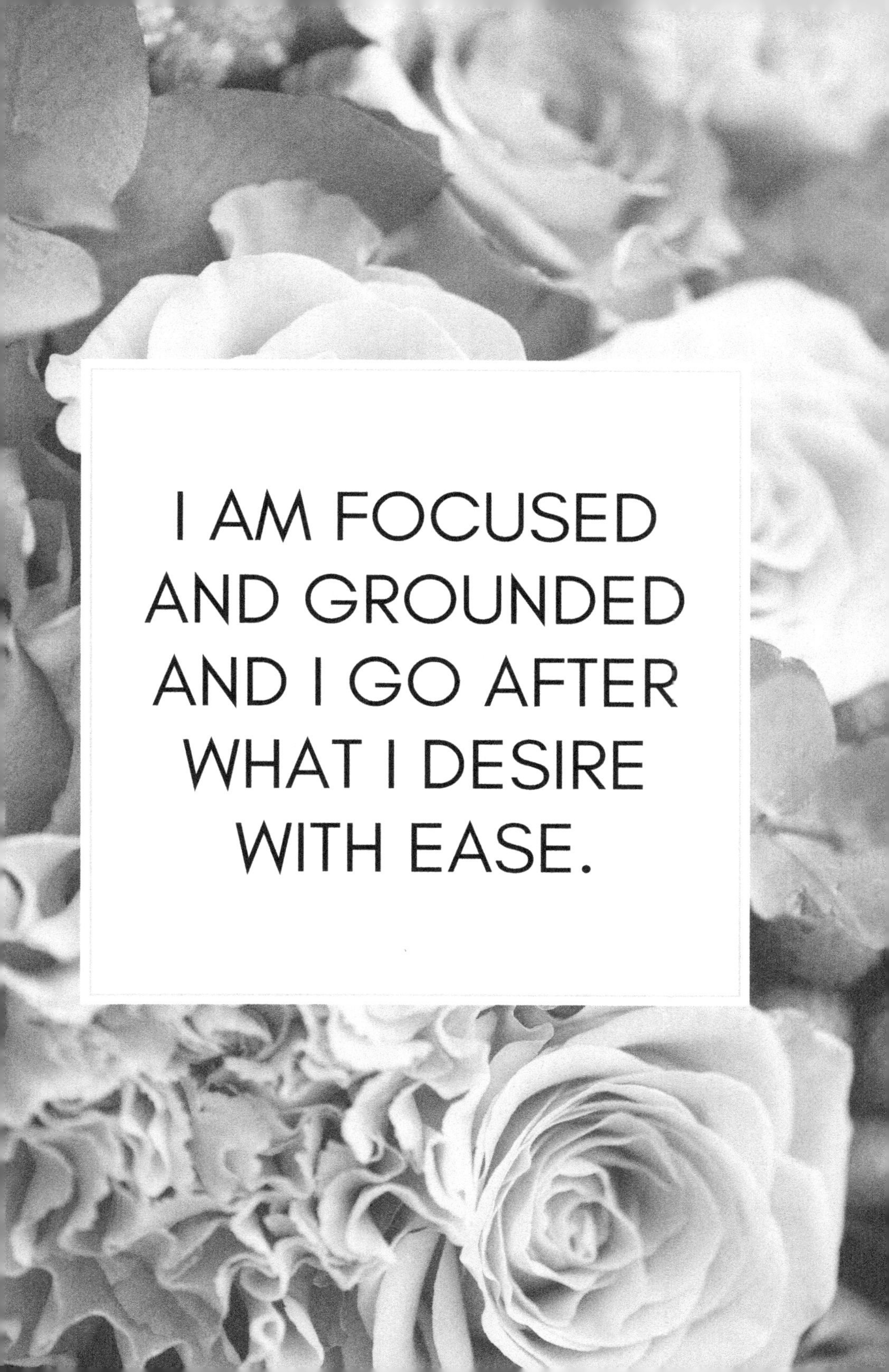
I AM FOCUSED
AND GROUNDED
AND I GO AFTER
WHAT I DESIRE
WITH EASE.

Date ______________________

Today I am excited about ______________________

A negative thought that I am changing today is ______________________

A new positive thought I am embrace today is ______________________

One word that describes me is ______________________

I Want to Manifest in My Life

(Describe in detail with visuals and senses)

Thoughts - Reflections - Manifestations

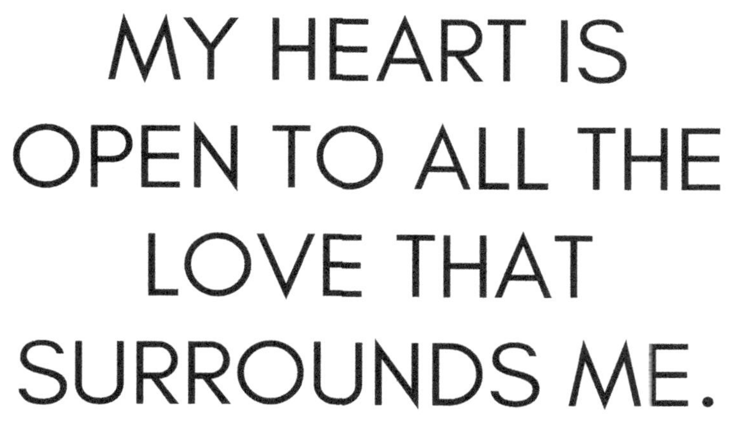

MY HEART IS OPEN TO ALL THE LOVE THAT SURROUNDS ME.

Date ____________________

I am always free to choose, and today I choose ____________

I have courage to say no to ____________

In this moment, I feel ____________

Each day I do my best to ____________

I Want to Manifest in My Life

(Describe in detail with visuals and senses)

Thoughts - Reflections - Manifestations

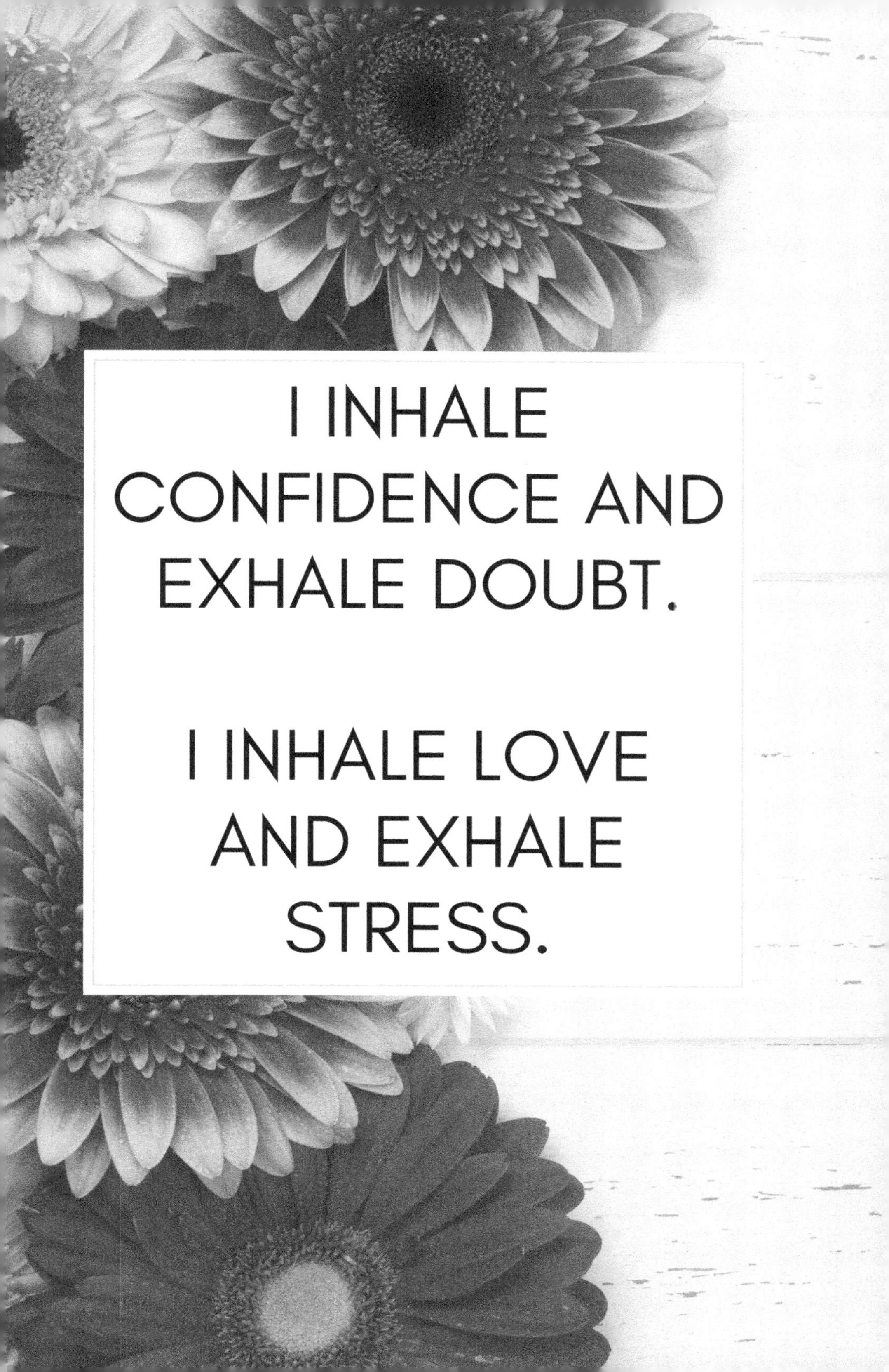
I INHALE
CONFIDENCE AND
EXHALE DOUBT.
I INHALE LOVE
AND EXHALE
STRESS.

Date ______________________

My favorite song is ______________________

Five years from now I will be ______________________

If I could stop time, I would ______________________

Last time I cried was when ______________________

I Want to Manifest in My Life

(Describe in detail with visuals and senses)

Thoughts - Reflections - Manifestations

I ALLOW MYSELF TO DREAM BIG. I AM WORTHY OF GREAT THINGS IN MY LIFE, AND I DESERVE A WONDERFUL FUTURE.

Date ______________________

I am proud of myself for ______________________

Today I am grateful for ______________________

One thing I do to make my body healthier is ______________________

Today I seek more knowledge in ______________________

I Want to Manifest in My Life

(Describe in detail with visuals and senses)

Thoughts - Reflections - Manifestations

I HAVE MY PAST, BUT IT DOES NOT DICTATE MY FUTURE. I CHOOSE TO CREATE THE LIFE I DESIRE.

Date

Today I choose to feel good about

I forgive myself for

Success means

People who love and support me are

I Want to Manifest in My Life

(Describe in detail with visuals and senses)

Thoughts - Reflections - Manifestations

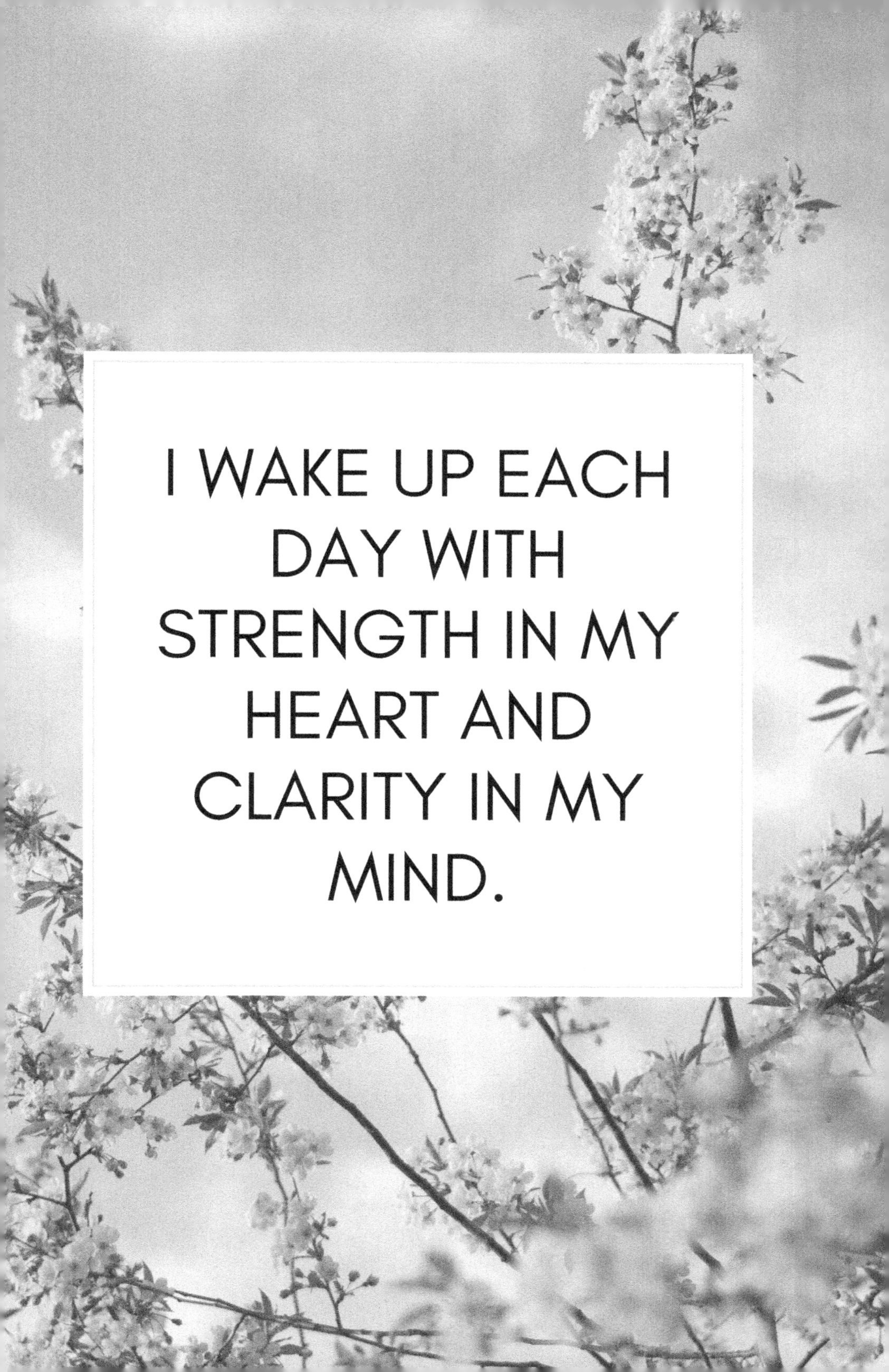
I WAKE UP EACH DAY WITH STRENGTH IN MY HEART AND CLARITY IN MY MIND.

Date ______________________

My uniqueness is ______________________

I believe in my ability to ______________________

One thing I am worthy of happening in my life is ______________________

Things that make my heart sing are ______________________

I Want to Manifest in My Life

(Describe in detail with visuals and senses)

Thoughts - Reflections - Manifestations

I GIVE MYSELF
PERMISSION TO
TAKE A BREAK FROM
THE BUSY LIFE AND
DO THINGS THAT
FILL MY HEART
WITH JOY.

Date ______________________

One thing I love doing is ______________________

Today I feel ______________________

A relationship I value most is ______________________

My greatest passion is ______________________

I Want to Manifest in My Life

(Describe in detail with visuals and senses)

Thoughts - Reflections - Manifestations

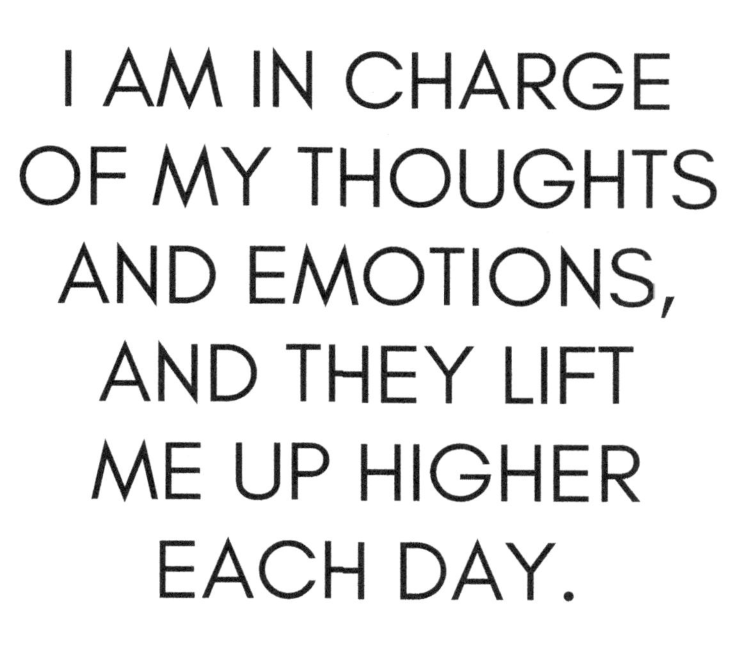
I AM IN CHARGE
OF MY THOUGHTS
AND EMOTIONS,
AND THEY LIFT
ME UP HIGHER
EACH DAY.

Date ______________________

Today's greatest fear I'm transforming into ______________

One thing I look forward to every day is ______________

Today I want ______________

I want to be a little more patient about ______________

I Want to Manifest in My Life

(Describe in detail with visuals and senses)

Thoughts - Reflections - Manifestations

I CHOOSE TO BE LOVING AND COMPASSIONATE TO MYSELF EVEN WHEN I MAKE MISTAKES. THIS IS THE TIME WHEN LOVE IS NEEDED MOST.

Date

Abundance I want to see today is

One thing I'll do today to step out of my comfort zone is

I feel confident when I do

My favorite act of kindness is

I Want to Manifest in My Life

(Describe in detail with visuals and senses)

Thoughts - Reflections - Manifestations

I ALWAYS DO MY BEST, AND THAT IS ENOUGH.

Date ______________________

A person I appreciate so much is ______________

5 things that make me smile today are ______________

One thing that is true to me no matter what is ______________

I am excellent at ______________

I Want to Manifest in My Life

(Describe in detail with visuals and senses)

Thoughts - Reflections - Manifestations

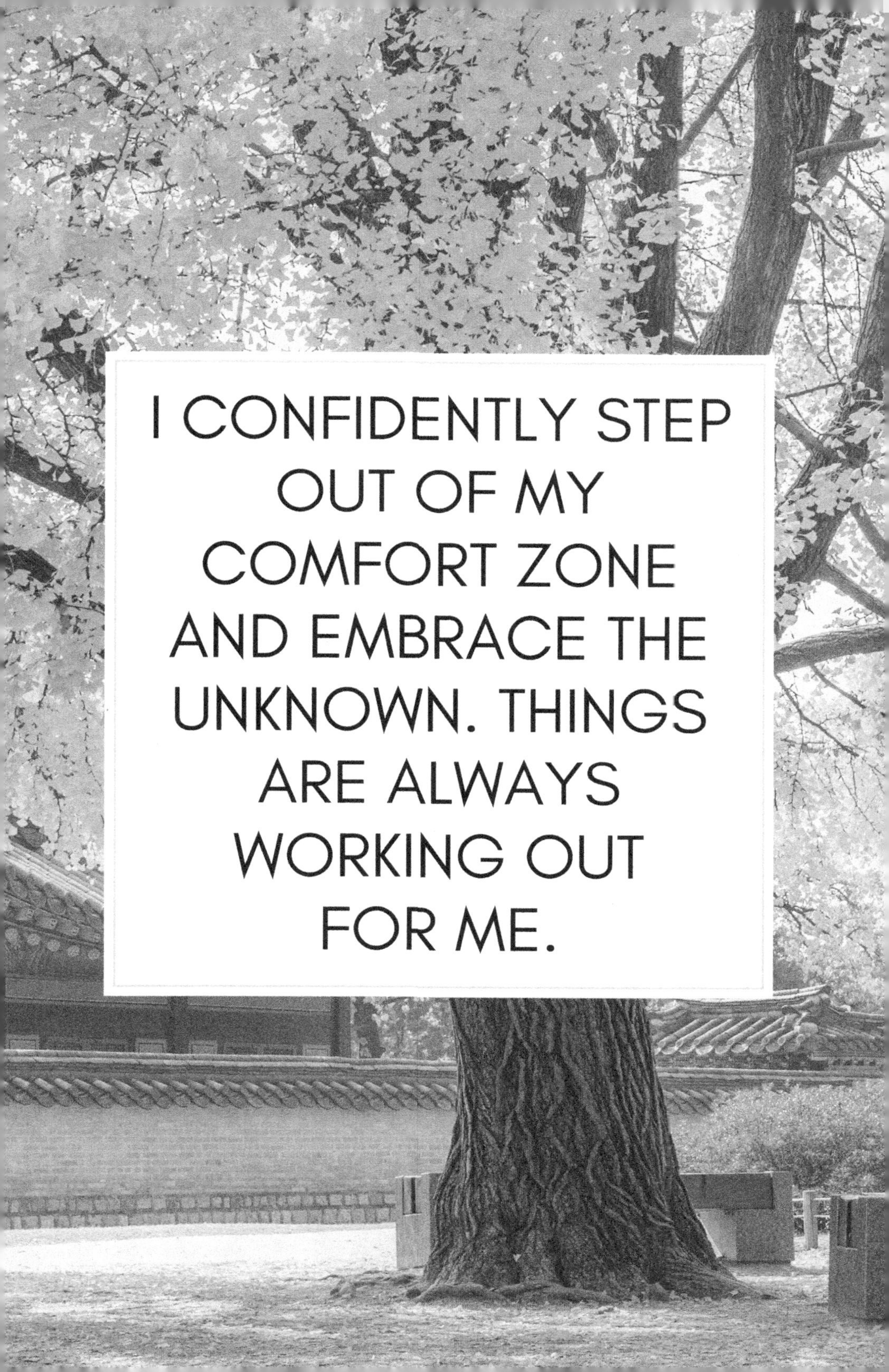
I CONFIDENTLY STEP
OUT OF MY
COMFORT ZONE
AND EMBRACE THE
UNKNOWN. THINGS
ARE ALWAYS
WORKING OUT
FOR ME.

Date

An opportunity I am looking for is

My purpose in life is

Today I'll start creating

True friendship means

I Want to Manifest in My Life

(Describe in detail with visuals and senses)

Thoughts - Reflections - Manifestations

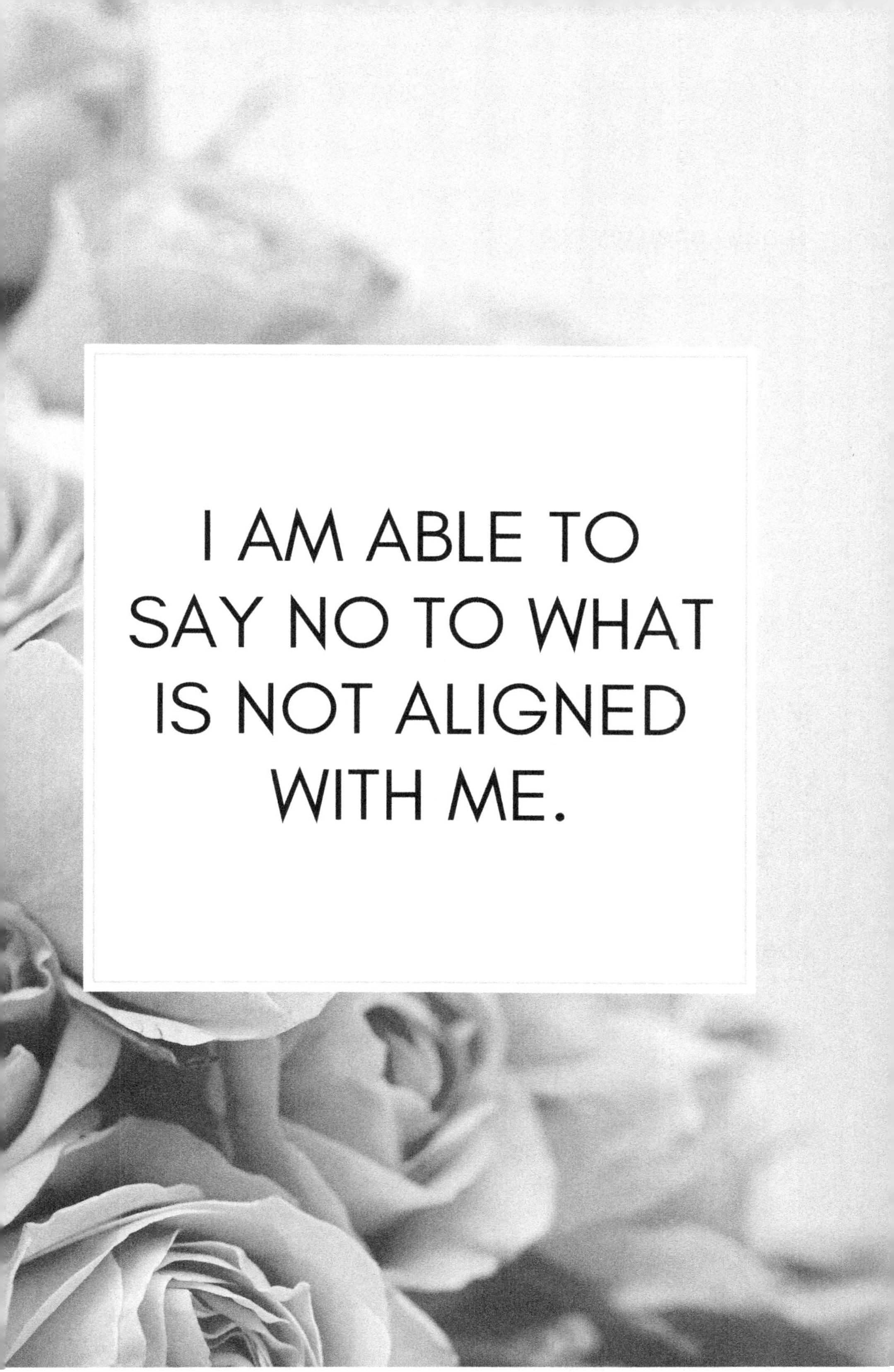
I AM ABLE TO
SAY NO TO WHAT
IS NOT ALIGNED
WITH ME.

Date

Today I open my heart to

I was born to be

My greatest strength is

I deserve happiness because

I Want to Manifest in My Life

(Describe in detail with visuals and senses)

Thoughts - Reflections - Manifestations

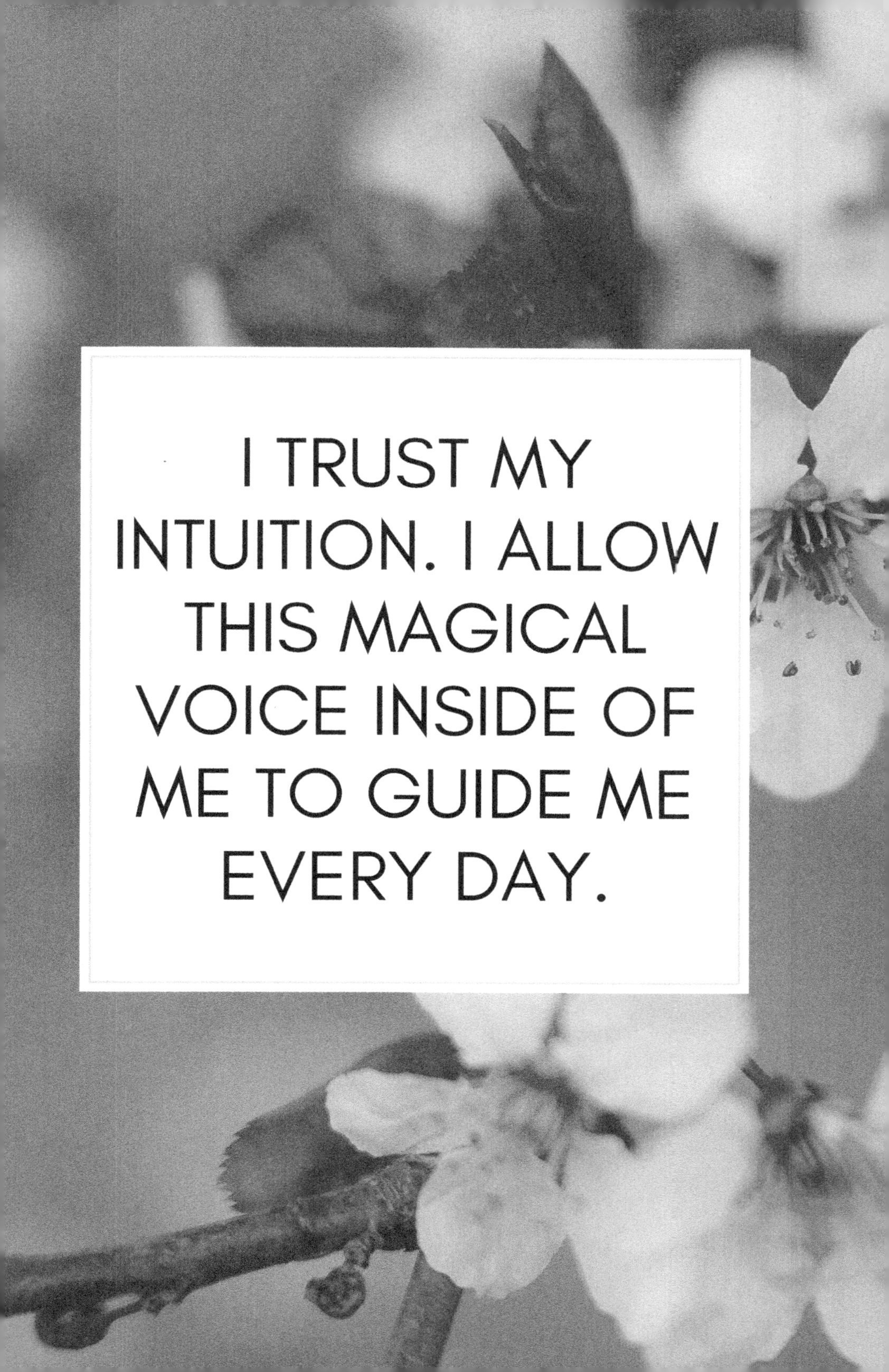
I TRUST MY
INTUITION. I ALLOW
THIS MAGICAL
VOICE INSIDE OF
ME TO GUIDE ME
EVERY DAY.

Date

Love is

My imperfection that I want to embrace is

A positive thought I'll focus on today is

One thing I want to change in the world is

I Want to Manifest in My Life

(Describe in detail with visuals and senses)

Thoughts - Reflections - Manifestations

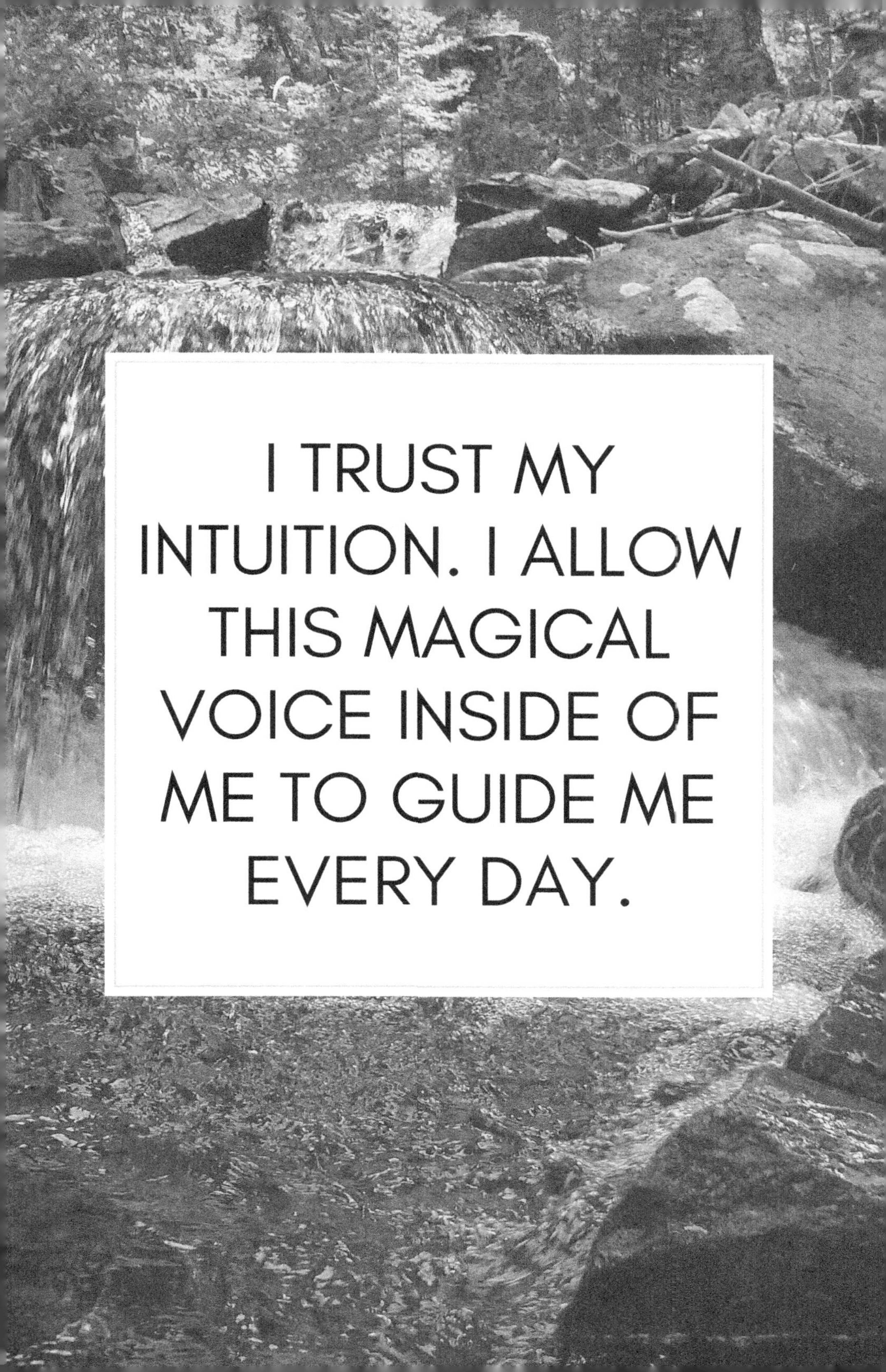
I TRUST MY INTUITION. I ALLOW THIS MAGICAL VOICE INSIDE OF ME TO GUIDE ME EVERY DAY.

Date

Something that brings me joy is

One thing I'd like to improve on is

I am so thankful for

I am most productive when

I Want to Manifest in My Life

(Describe in detail with visuals and senses)

Thoughts - Reflections - Manifestations

I LOVE AND
ACCEPT MY BODY
AND MY HEIGHT,
MY WEIGHT, AND
ALL MY CURVES.

Date

Something I'd like to learn is

Today I'm grateful for

Last time I laughed about was

I dare to dream about

I Want to Manifest in My Life

(Describe in detail with visuals and senses)

Thoughts ~ Reflections ~ Manifestations

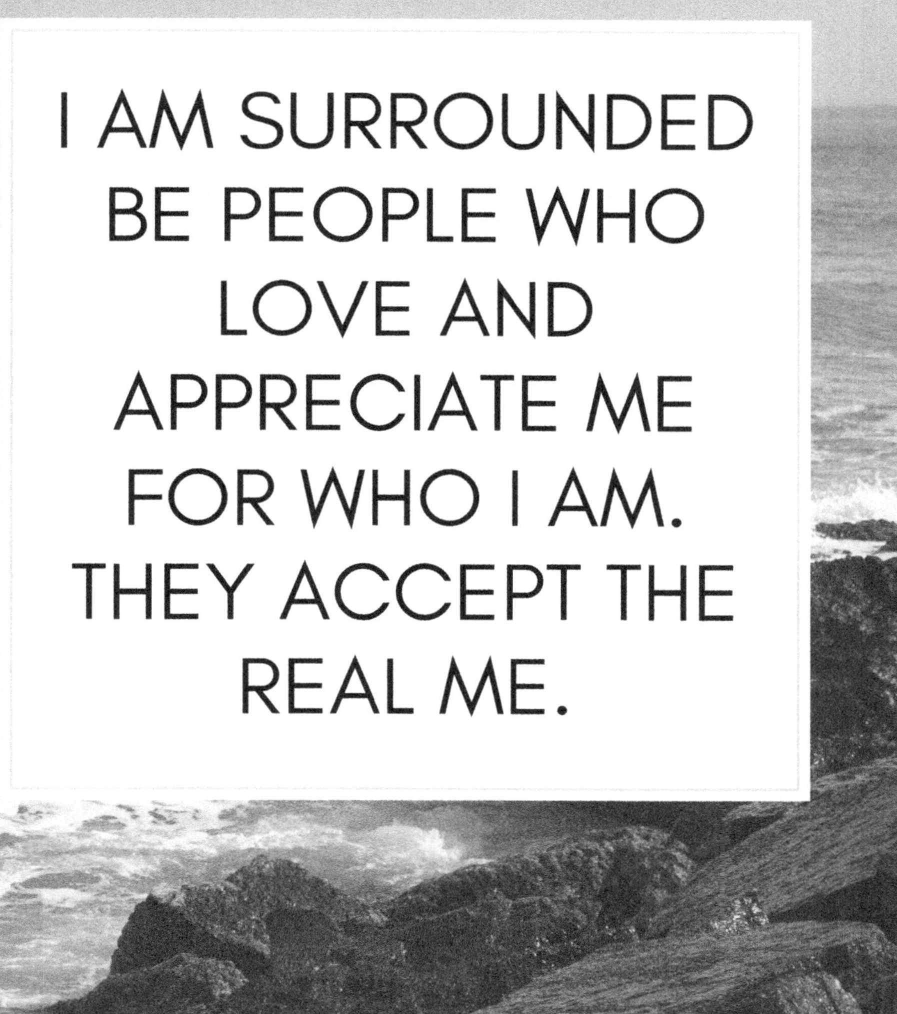
I AM SURROUNDED
BE PEOPLE WHO
LOVE AND
APPRECIATE ME
FOR WHO I AM.
THEY ACCEPT THE
REAL ME.

Date

If I knew then what I know now, I would

I allow myself to dream big because

Every day I become better at

My biggest goal is

I Want to Manifest in My Life

(Describe in detail with visuals and senses)

Thoughts - Reflections - Manifestations

MY VOICE IS
POWERFUL. MY
VOICE MATTERS.

Date

Today I'll express my appreciation to

If I could do anything for work, I would

Boundaries that need to get stronger are

Someone I admire is

I Want to Manifest in My Life

(Describe in detail with visuals and senses)

Thoughts - Reflections - Manifestations

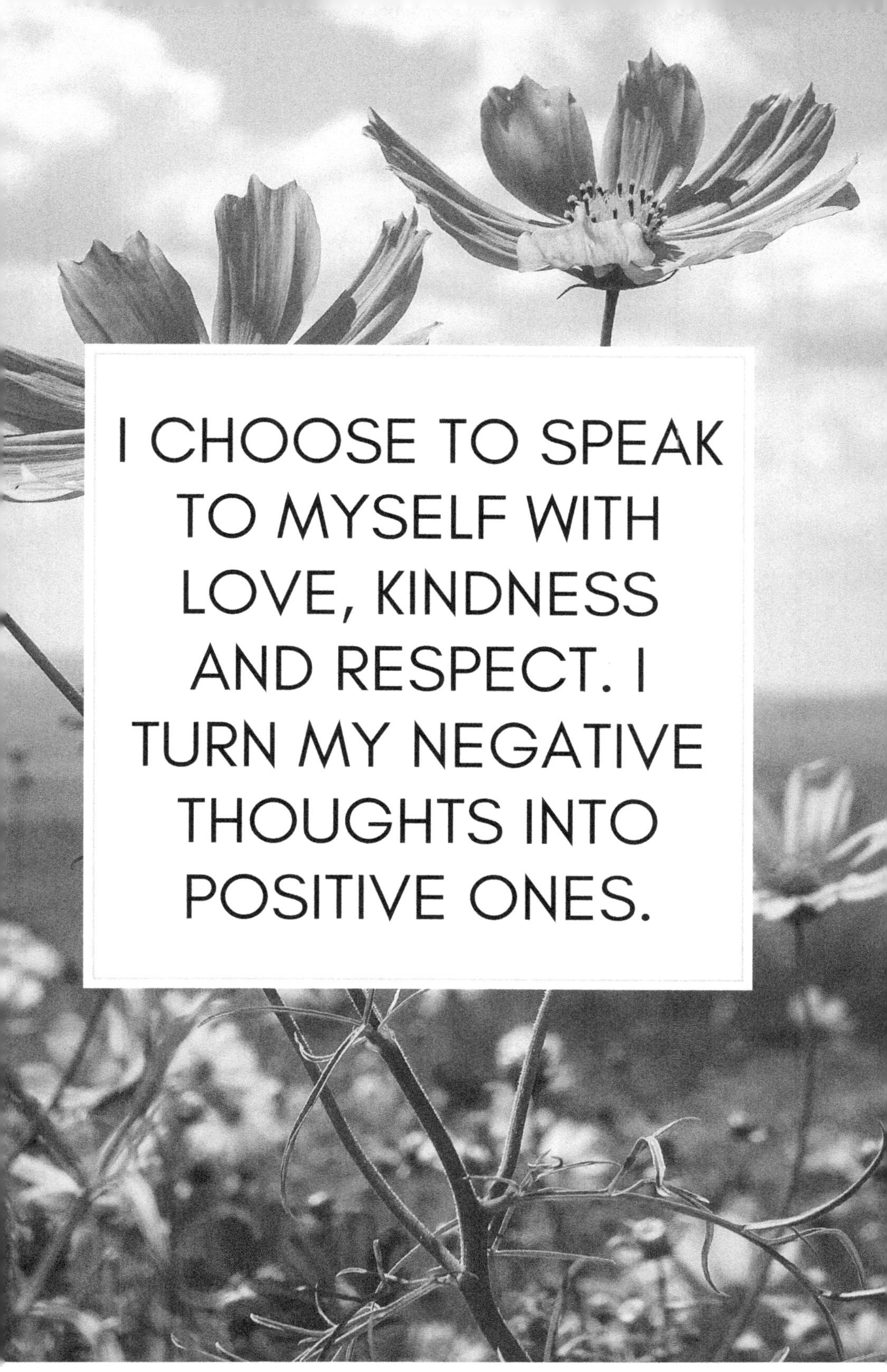
I CHOOSE TO SPEAK
TO MYSELF WITH
LOVE, KINDNESS
AND RESPECT. I
TURN MY NEGATIVE
THOUGHTS INTO
POSITIVE ONES.

Date

The way I can extend compassion to myself is

If I could travel to any country, I'd go to

Something I'd like others to learn from me is

A person I trust most is

I Want to Manifest in My Life

(Describe in detail with visuals and senses)

Thoughts - Reflections - Manifestations

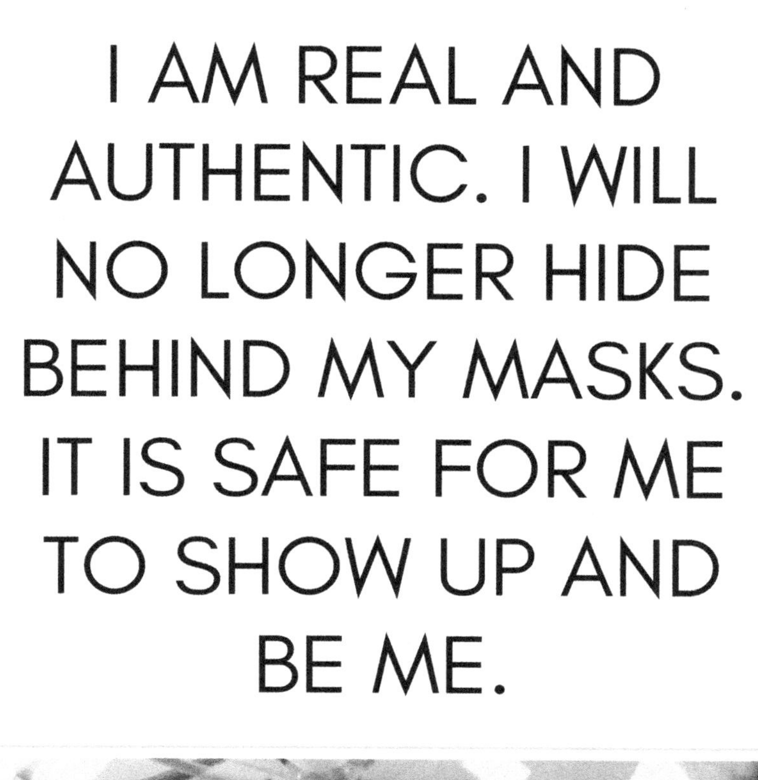
I AM REAL AND
AUTHENTIC. I WILL
NO LONGER HIDE
BEHIND MY MASKS.
IT IS SAFE FOR ME
TO SHOW UP AND
BE ME.

Date ______________________

The way I could better support my loved ones is ______

3 things I'd like to share with my friends ______

The most important thing to me is ______

My life would be incomplete without ______

I Want to Manifest in My Life

(Describe in detail with visuals and senses)

Thoughts ~ Reflections ~ Manifestations

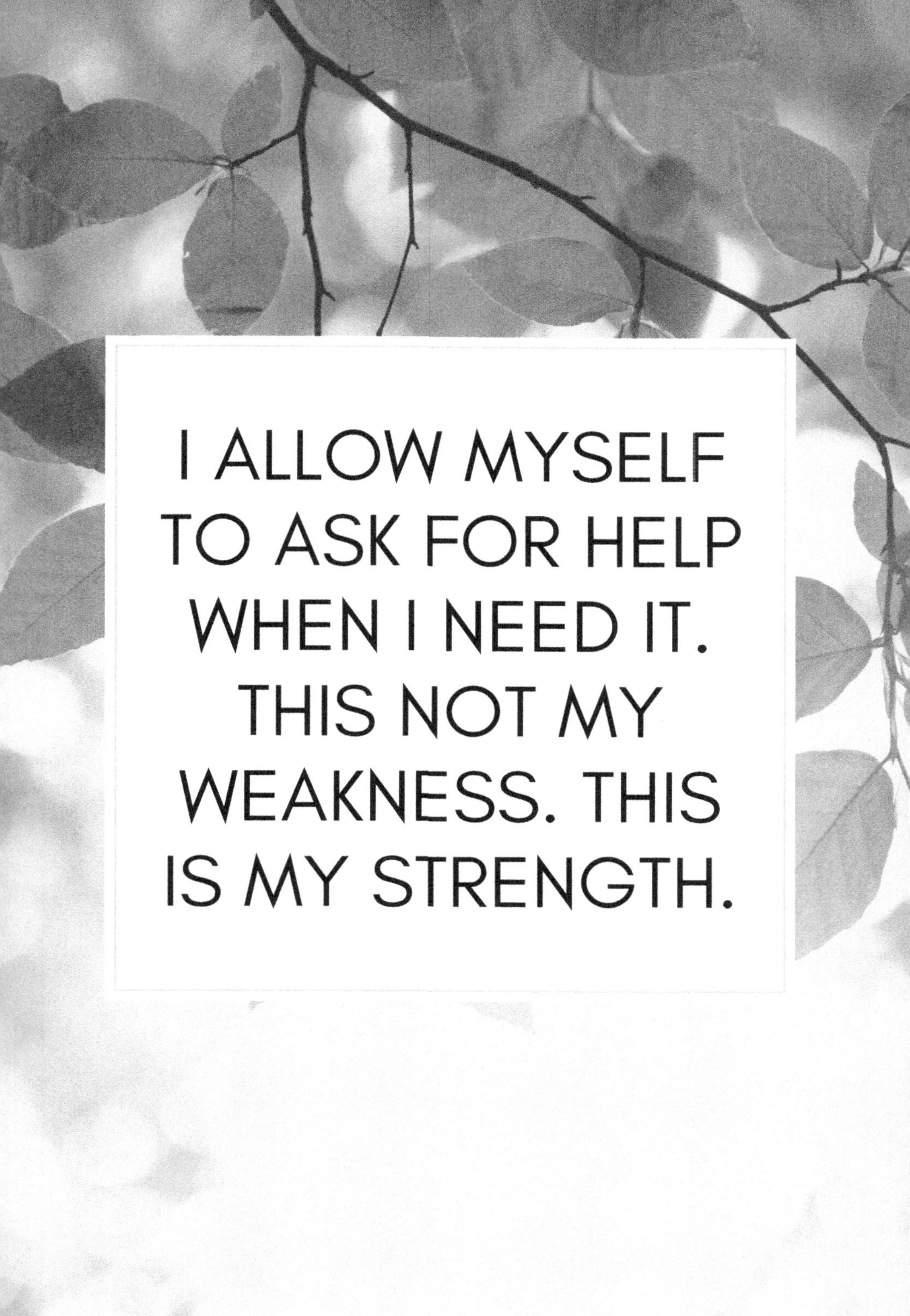
I ALLOW MYSELF
TO ASK FOR HELP
WHEN I NEED IT.
THIS NOT MY
WEAKNESS. THIS
IS MY STRENGTH.

Date ______________________

Something that shaped me into who I am today is ______

____

____

____

One thing that I love about my friends is ______

____

____

____

An emotion that I find hard to accept is ______

____

____

____

I'll show appreciation to myself by ______

____

____

____

I Want to Manifest in My Life

(Describe in detail with visuals and senses)

Thoughts ~ Reflections ~ Manifestations

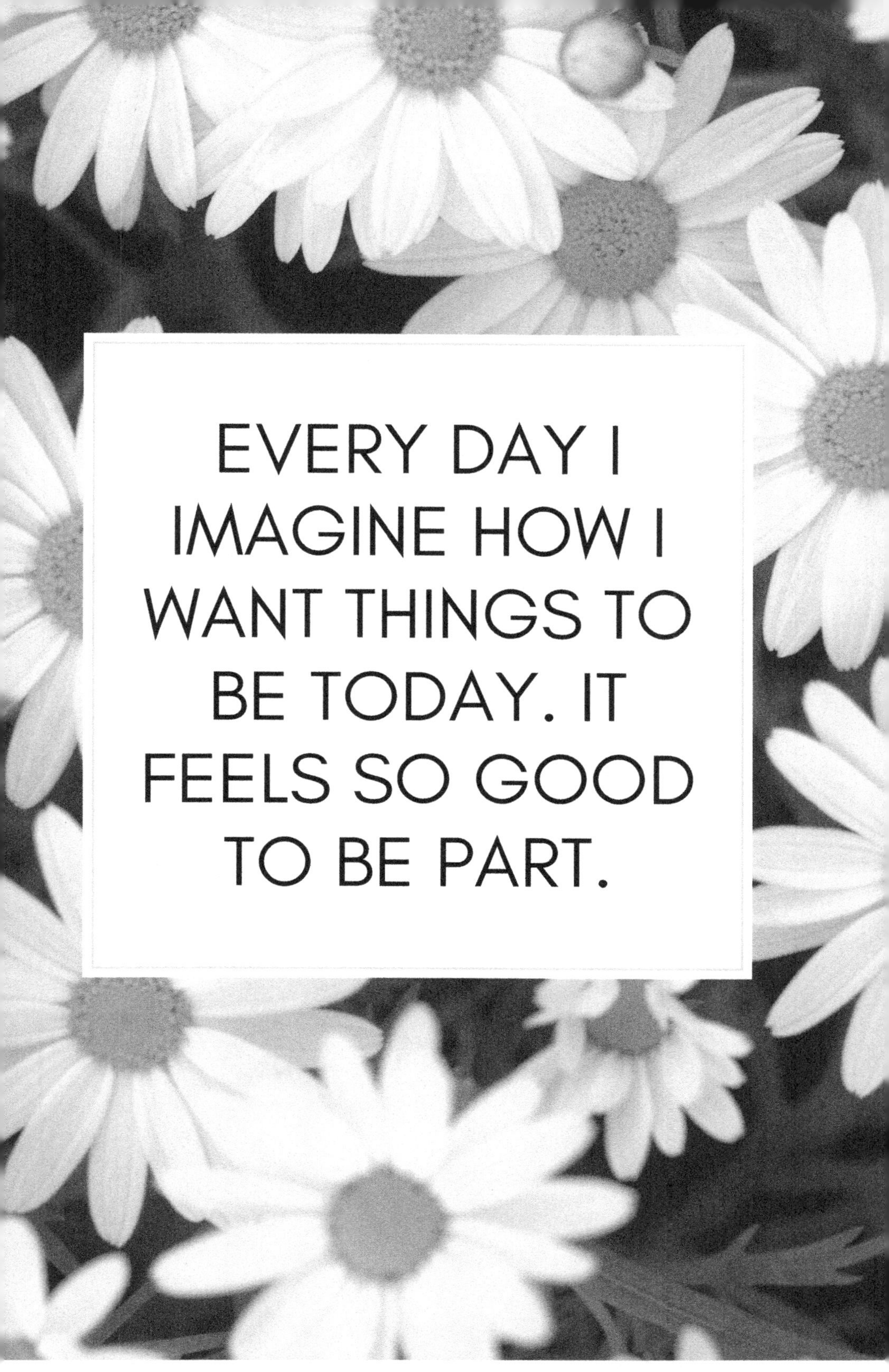
EVERY DAY I
IMAGINE HOW I
WANT THINGS TO
BE TODAY. IT
FEELS SO GOOD
TO BE PART.

Date

Something I can do when I feel low is

A simple thing that brings me joy is

Today I can relax by

My favorite hobby is

I Want to Manifest in My Life

(Describe in detail with visuals and senses)

Thoughts ~ Reflections ~ Manifestations

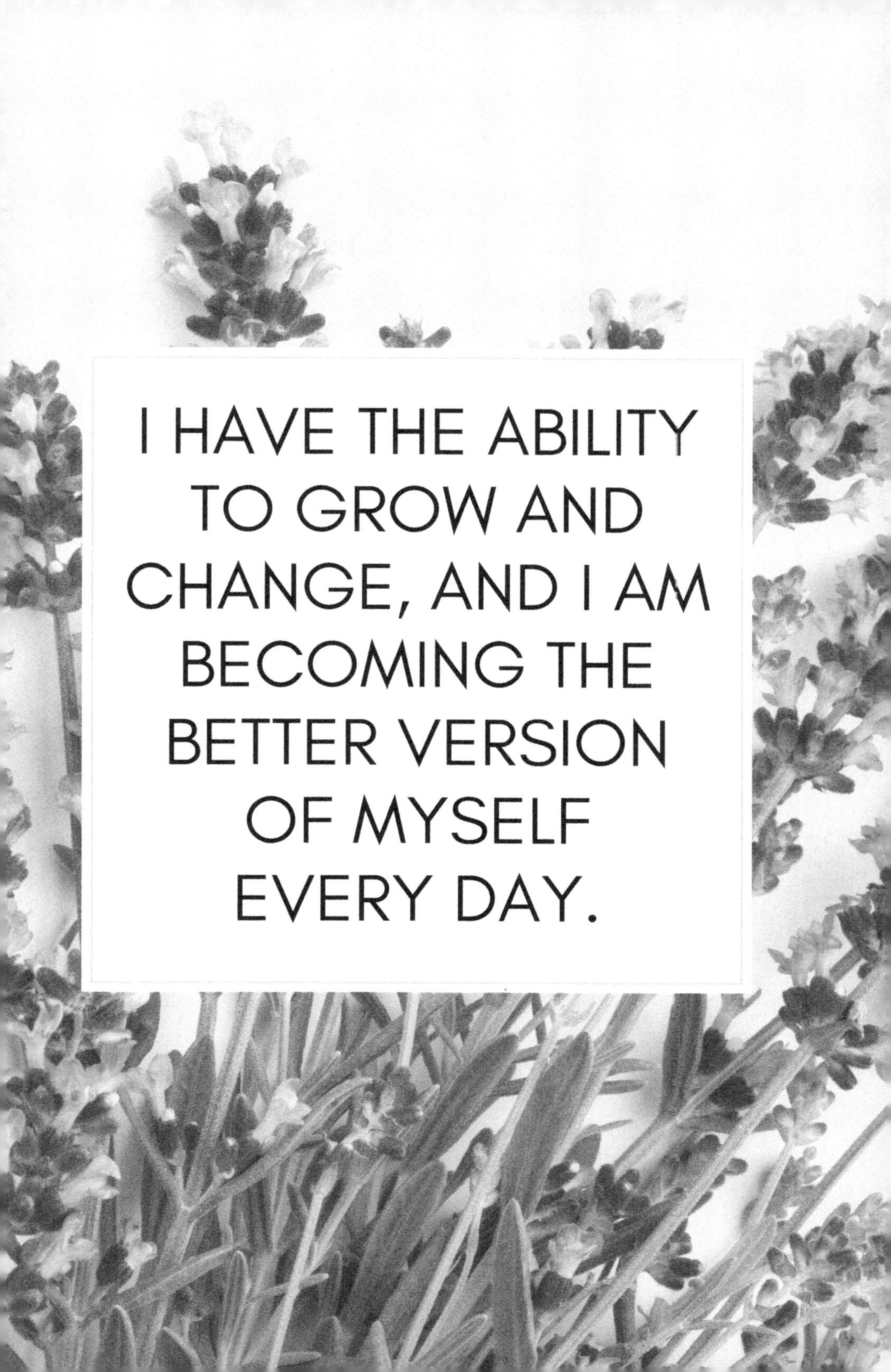
I HAVE THE ABILITY
TO GROW AND
CHANGE, AND I AM
BECOMING THE
BETTER VERSION
OF MYSELF
EVERY DAY.

Date ______________________________

A place that makes me feel most peaceful is ____________

I can change my sadness to ______________________________

My top 3 values are ______________________________

The way I could appreciate my loved ones is ____________

I Want to Manifest in My Life

(Describe in detail with visuals and senses)

Thoughts ~ Reflections ~ Manifestations

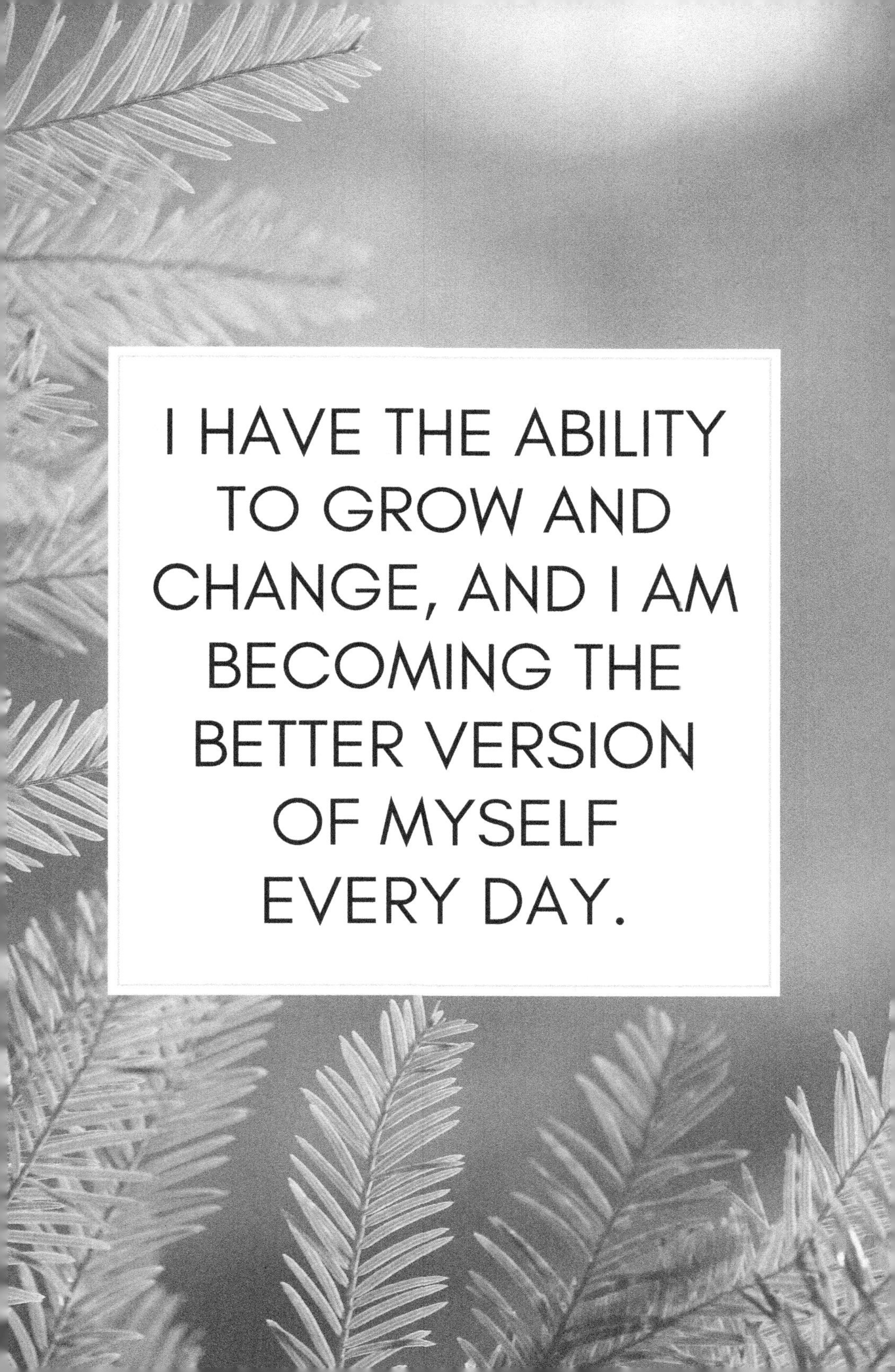
I HAVE THE ABILITY
TO GROW AND
CHANGE, AND I AM
BECOMING THE
BETTER VERSION
OF MYSELF
EVERY DAY.

Date

Something that surprised me is

One thing I'd share with my younger self is

A goal that I have accomplished is

One thing that helps me stay focused is

I Want to Manifest in My Life

(Describe in detail with visuals and senses)

Thoughts - Reflections - Manifestations

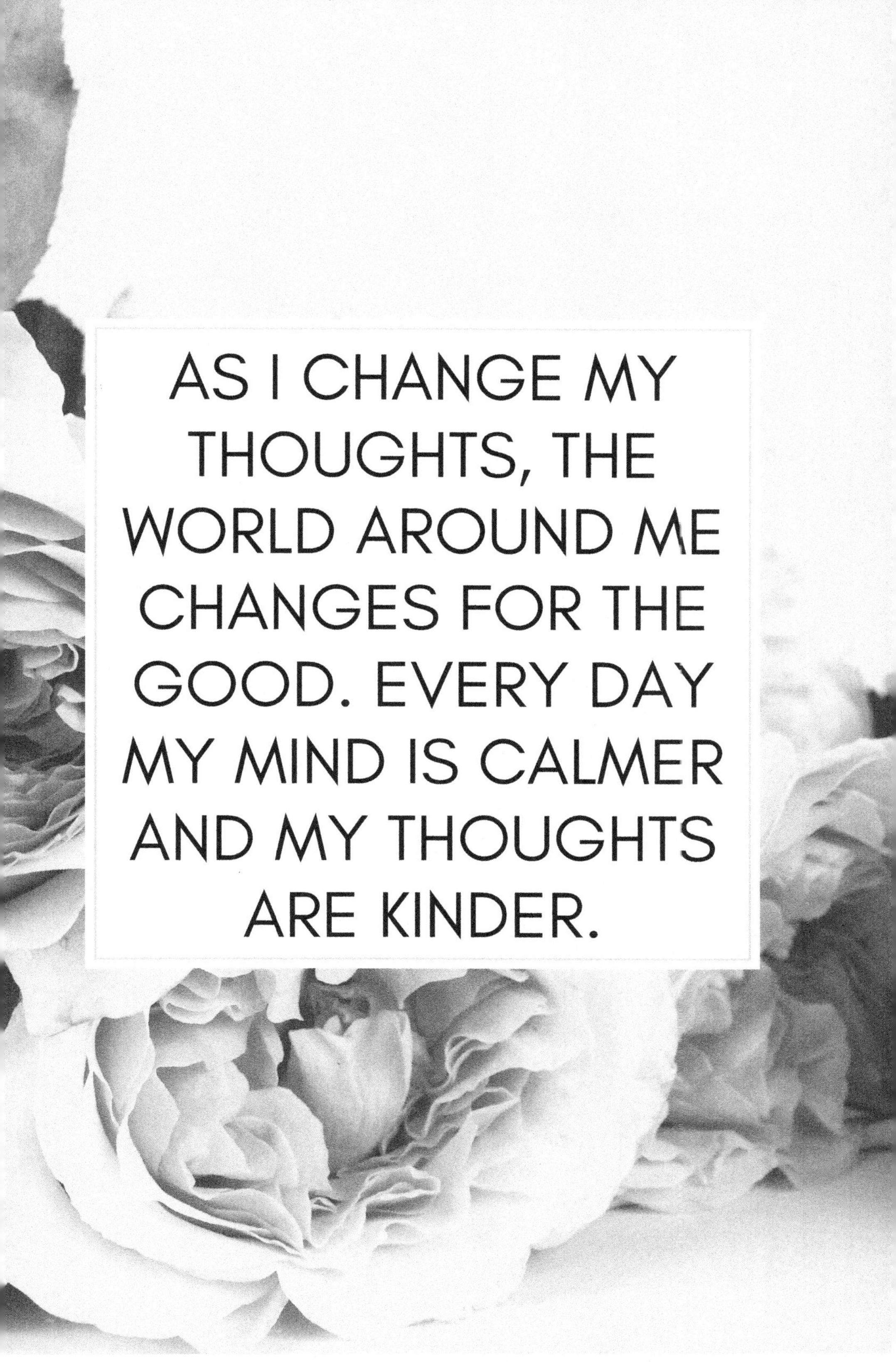
AS I CHANGE MY THOUGHTS, THE WORLD AROUND ME CHANGES FOR THE GOOD. EVERY DAY MY MIND IS CALMER AND MY THOUGHTS ARE KINDER.

Date ______________________

I truly desire to ______________________

Something that brings me joy is ______________________

Today I look forward to ______________________

I'll always be grateful to ______________________

I Want to Manifest in My Life

(Describe in detail with visuals and senses)

Thoughts ~ Reflections ~ Manifestations

Made in the USA
Columbia, SC
23 October 2024